The Self in Social Work

LIBRARY OF SOCIAL WORK

GENERAL EDITOR: NOEL TIMMS

Professor of Applied Social Studies
University of Bradford

The Self in Social Work

John Shaw

Extra-Mural Department
University of Manchester

HV
41
S43

Routledge & Kegan Paul

London and Boston

First published in 1974
by Routledge & Kegan Paul Ltd
Broadway House, 68-74 Carter Lane
London EC4V 5EL and
9 Park Street,
Boston, Mass. 02108, USA
Set in ten point Pilgrim on twelve point body
and printed in Great Britain by
Northumberland Press Limited, Gateshead
© John Shaw 1974
ISBN 0 7100 7920 6 (c)
      0 7100 7921 4 (p)
Library of Congress Catalog Card No. 74-80104

General editor's introduction

The Library of Social Work is designed to meet the needs of students following courses of training for social work. In recent years the number and kinds of training have increased in an unprecedented way. The Library will consist of short texts designed to introduce the student to the main features of each topic of enquiry, to the significant theoretical contributions so far made to its understanding, and to some of the outstanding problems. Each volume will suggest ways in which the student might continue his work by further reading.

This study of theorising about the self and the implications of such theorising for social work begins by recognising the contemporary criticism of many of the value-laden terms used in social work—terms like wholeness, growth and adjustment. It is the author's argument that 'it is the experience of self-actualisation which could give the social worker more confidence in rebutting the assertions of some clients that normal social adjustment is simply the road to deadness, unreality, or the treadmill of normal working life'. He follows this argument through a consideration of the model of the life cycle as a basis for social work intervention, emphasising that it is the whole of life that should be spanned by the cycle and not simply the earlier stages. He then examines the self-concept and theories of self-actualisation in the work of a range of authors (Maslow, Rogers, Jung and others). Their views support his arguments that a human desire of self-realisation and a personality-type called the self-actualising person can be identified. Some of these theories are assessed in chapter 4, whilst chapters 3 and 5 are basically concerned with methods of fostering self-actualisation and the implications of self-theory for social work.

The subject of this monograph is not often discussed in connection with social work, but, as John Shaw makes clear, it has considerable relevance. Theorising about the self-concept and about self-actualisation can be seen as contributing to the knowledge base of social work. The book deals with a subject which is complex in itself and which touches on other questions of considerable difficulty (e.g. the concept of need, the distinction between 'is' and 'ought' statements). The theoretical issues are not baulked, but the author, because of his very subject-matter, is equally concerned with the use made of the concepts and theories. As in many other areas of social work knowledge the theorising has direct relevance for the social worker as well as for the client. The reader is shown a range of theorising which agrees on the importance of the self-concept and the work of Rogers, coming once again into critical pre-eminence, is substantially discussed to show how theorising and practice go together. As the author says: 'This book is a contribution to knowledge, and the usefulness of this *knowledge* in assisting the social worker in his *understanding* of the unique individuals with whom he or she is confronted can only be decided by each worker's own practical experience.'

NOEL TIMMS

Contents

CONTENTS

viii

Illustrations

Acknowledgments

My thanks are due to the Editor of the series for his help and guidance; to Mr Ralph Ruddock for reading the typescript and suggesting many useful improvements to the text; to Hazel Gordon and Pat Moneypenny for providing the typescript so readily, despite the many other demands on them; and to Hodder & Stoughton for permission to use the figures on pages 4-7.

J.W.S.

Manchester

Introduction

Recent writers on social work have rightly pointed out that social work needs to be placed in a political and sociological framework. Without wishing to deny the validity of this standpoint, this book aims to concentrate on the basic *raison d'être* of social work, the individual client. What, it may be asked, do we still need to know about the individual client, considering that this has been one of the major preoccupations of social work training this long time? This book is my attempt to answer this question.

In her article (1972, p. 253), Crescy Cannan quotes the following sentence from an introduction to social work and underlines it as an example of 'wishy-washy thinking', *'There is a natural tendency in all living things to strive towards wholeness and normality'*. She goes on to comment that this sentence and the paragraph in which it is located are 'full of completely unjustified beliefs about the characteristics of the "client" and about the "natural" order of things. The bland assertions of "natural tendencies" are simply a crude way of legitimising the social workers' intervention.'

It is true that statements like this are used in the service of wishy-washy thinking or are asserted blandly. But in this book there will be an attempt to show that a number of workers in the human sciences have been struck by such a 'natural tendency' in the human organism and have succeeded in expressing very coherently how they understand this 'natural tendency' to work and what they consider its main aspects to be.

In the above quotation 'wholeness and normality' are coupled together and Crescy Cannan says of this (ibid.):

Terms like 'immaturity', 'growth', 'adjustment', cannot possibly be said to be value-free, especially since the social-work agency is concerned with the modification of behaviour in the direction of certain (dominant) norms. If the *status quo* is presented as natural and normal, then deviation or criticism is by definition unnatural and abnormal. The definition of abnormality thus depends on one of normality which is never itself questioned or justified.

Cannan thus raises a crucial issue in social work but decides that social work, as normally practised, is expected to be a means whereby 'straight' society rounds up its erring members and puts them back on the path followed by the majority. In an earlier discussion of this problem, I said (Shaw, 1972, p. 141):

It is likely that the social workers whose main concern is with helping socially maladjusted clients to take a regular job, accept family responsibilities and become a normal member of society will see difficulties in the notion of self-actualisation. For one is struck, in reading the evidence for self-actualisation, by the independence and autonomy which it fosters in individuals. Self-actualisation, if widely experienced, might begin to overturn social norms and prevailing values, and jeopardise the goals that the social worker has for his clients.

But, in fact, normal social adjustment is usually the foundation upon which the self-actualising person builds his further development. He does not deny normal social values but has a drive to transcend them. There is, however, in modern urban society, the problem of 'alienation', a term used by Marx and also by existentialists to describe the experience of separation from fellow man, society, nature and oneself. The evidence from the self-actualising person holds out hope that individuals in a modern urban society may be able to 're-appropriate' these relationships. It is the experience of self-actualisation which could give the social worker more confidence in rebutting the assertions of some clients that normal social adjustment is simply the road to deadness, unreality, or the treadmill of normal working life.

It is along these lines that the study of self-actualisation theories, outlined in the following pages, has something to offer in resolving the moral dilemma of social work, which is so clearly indicated by Cannan.

Another problem arises from the relationship between *knowledge* and *understanding*. Writers on self-actualisation emphasise the *unique* development of the individual but nevertheless wish to talk about this idea in general (i.e. scientific) terms. Jung (1958a, pp. 9-10) puts this dilemma very well:

> it is not the universal and the regular that characterise the individual, but rather the unique. He is not to be understood as a recurrent unit but as something unique and singular which in the last analysis can neither be known nor compared with anything else. At the same time man, as a member of a species, can and must be described as a statistical unit; otherwise nothing general could be said about him. For this purpose he has to be regarded as a comparative unit. This results in a universally valid anthropology or psychology, as the case may be, with an abstract picture of man as an average unit from which all individual features have been removed. But it is precisely these features which are of paramount importance for *understanding* man. If I want to understand an individual human being, I must lay aside all scientific knowledge of the average man and discard all theories in order to adopt a completely new and unprejudiced attitude. I can only approach the task of *understanding* with a free and open mind, whereas *knowledge* of man, or insight into human character, presupposes all sorts of knowledge about mankind in general.

In discussing, as this book does, self-actualisation as a psychological concept, we are talking in terms of knowledge *not* understanding. Social work, as I see it, is about *understanding* the individual, rather than knowledge about people in general. This book is a contribution to knowledge, and the usefulness of this *knowledge* in assisting the social worker in his *understanding* of the unique individuals with whom he or she is confronted can only be decided by each worker's own practical experience.

I

Human developmental forces as the basis for social work intervention

Introduction

Most people in the helping professions are familiar with the idea of successive stages in human development. We have, for example, Freud's analysis into oral, anal, genital, latency and pubertal stages (modified by later psychoanalytical thinkers but not substantially changed). Also, Piaget has charted intellectual development through adualism, dualism and animism, followed by the acquisition of concrete operational logic at about the age of seven, and finally, at about twelve, the acquisition of abstract logical ability. Some psychological writers, notably Erikson, have charted successive stages throughout the whole life-cycle, but in the main, the preoccupation has been with the stages up to, and including, adolescence. Perhaps this emphasis on the early stages of emotional and intellectual life has been necessary to give the study of human development a firm foundation.

However, the human organism has a life of about 65 to 75 years. And the clients dealt with by social workers are at all stages of the life-cycle from infancy to old age. The aim of this first chapter is to explore the extent of our present knowledge about this life-cycle and its developmental pattern; for there is no reason to believe *a priori* that psycho-social development stops when the young adult has successfully adapted to the demands of work, sex, and personal and social relationships. To put it another way, there seems no reason why the emotional and intellectual maturation processes which are seen to unfold with remarkable dynamism in the first twenty or so years of life should suddenly exhaust themselves or simply remain constant for many years until old age sets in.

A model of the life-cycle

If we plot human life as a curve (see Figure 1), we can with some justice, and not too much distortion, point to a number of life-stages that have a characteristic psycho-social 'flavour'. In Figure 1, these stages are marked off in terms of chronological age, but these can only be approximate, given the wide variation observed from individual to individual.

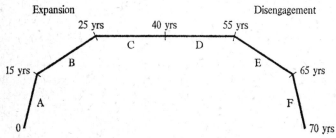

All ages quoted are only approximate.

Stage A Infancy and childhood
Stage B Adolescence and early adulthood
Stage C Young adulthood
Stage D Early middle age
Stage E Late middle age
Stage F Old age

FIGURE 1   *A model of the life-cycle*

(a) The period of infancy and childhood is, from the overall point of view, the period of preparation, development and learning. On the social and emotional side, it is characterised by an ever-expanding number of relationships, and an ever-growing acquisition of roles and group membership.

(b) In adolescence and early adulthood, the *expansion* of roles and relationships continues apace and the successful transition from childhood to adulthood is the individual's overriding preoccupation. A feature of transitional states is that regression often takes place, hence the asocial behaviour of this stage which is a cause of concern to the adult members of the population. Social activity reaches

2

its highest point and, in our culture, serves the two main goals of establishing oneself in one's job and finding a suitable marriage partner.

(c) Young adulthood: This stage has been called 'the period of maximum responsibility'. The social and economic demands upon the individual are considerable. The majority of young adults are married with children; their family roles and responsibilities are central to their lives. At the same time the need to make progress in job or career is imperative. Physically, the demands of home and work together are considerable; also, the young adult is often a member of a number of leisure, educational and career-oriented groups.

(d) Early middle age: For many individuals, this is often a period of fulfilment, in which the earlier struggles begin to reap some reward and the peak of job—or career—achievement is reached. At the same time, family roles change, with the growth and independence of children. Emotional changes take place in the mid- and late-forties, which are related to the physical changes taking place. Reproductive capacity begins to decline and may cease in the female in the late-forties but continue for a while longer in the male.

(e) Late middle age: While career-fulfilment may continue until retirement, peak performance is now over for many, and the *expansion* which characterises the earlier stages of the cycle is replaced by processes of *disengagement*, which may have begun earlier with the removal of the active parent role. The process of disengagement (i.e. concentration on fewer roles and activities) makes sense in that the individual is able to husband his or her scarcer physical resources. For the male, complete disengagement from the work-role comes suddenly with retirement, often with a sense of great loss to self-esteem. For the married female without an outside career, the disengagement process is slower, say, from the mid-forties on, and, therefore, for some, less traumatic.

(f) Old age: While many retired people retain the physical characteristics of late middle age, old age is the inevitable final stage of the cycle for all who survive to the full term of years. The emotional problems of such people, in our culture, often relate to coping with economic stringency, loneliness and boredom. For these reasons, some continuation of work and social relations fosters a sense of belonging, usefulness and happiness. While *disengagement* has its value, the need is to prevent the processes of disengagement going too far. Hence, as internal arousal is less, external stimulation has to be greater and may take the form of better incentives to activity, better facilities, persuasion and support. Also, the individual who plans for a certain amount of involvement and interaction will often retain greater physical and mental health.

As Erikson (see p. 16 below) and others have noted, the later stages of life necessitate a turning from outer activity to inner reflection. We might call this a greater preoccupation with the religious or spiritual or, more directly, a greater concern with the meaning of one's own individual existence. Individuals often tend to look back on their lives and try to evaluate them. They ask themselves, perhaps: did I accomplish my goals? Was my marriage and family life all I hoped it would be? Did I achieve all the things in my job I hoped I would? Erikson suggests that satisfactorily working through this personal assessment is essentially the purpose of the later, and particularly the last, stages of life. Charlotte Bühler's attempt to collect empirical data about the spiritual aspect of existence is discussed in the following section.

Bühler's spiritual-psychic ground-plan

Bühler (1933) carried out an investigation based on the completion of questionnaires by respondents who were themselves in the later years of life. She also collected during her research a considerable

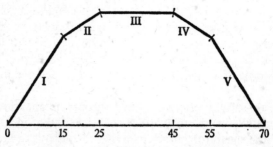

FIGURE 2 *The biological ground-plan*

4

amount of biographical data. On the basis of a careful analysis of these data, she found a number of *recurring patterns of concern with the spiritual and psychological aspects of life and was able to suggest a number of 'spiritual-psychic' life models that would illustrate these differences. To make her point, she then super-imposed these on a basic biological ground-plan.*

Bühler's 'biological ground-plan' is similar in many respects to the model of the life-cycle we considered in the previous section. It is illustrated here in Figure 2. It can be seen that she divides the biological ground-plan into five stages:

Stage   I   from 1 to 15 years
Stage II from 15 to 25 years
Stage III from 25 to 45 years
Stage IV from 45 to 55 years
Stage V from 55 to 70 years

Stages II and IV are transitional stages. They signal a change of direction biologically in that in Stage II reproductive capacity sets in, and in Stage IV it ceases. From the biological point of view, Bühler sees life as essentially expansive up to the age of forty-five, and as restrictive from then on until death.

Bühler discovered from her research that the simple biological ground-plan (Figure 2) would suffice to explain the lives of some individuals. For some individuals, and perhaps some would say for a good many, there is no reflective element. Life is simply lived spontaneously and vitally.

The most commonly observed pattern is illustrated in Figure 3.

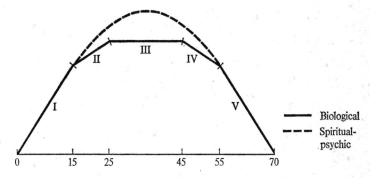

FIGURE 3 *The most commonly observed pattern.*
The spiritual-psychic coincides with the biological.
Both reach their peak in Stage III

5

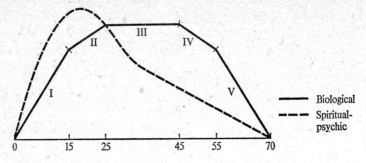

FIGURE 4 *The peak of the spiritual occurs in Stage II*
(These figures are to be found in J. Jacobi's *The Way of*
Individuation, Hodder & Stoughton (1967))

Here the spiritual-psychic curve is shown by a dotted line super-
imposed on the basic biological ground-plan of Figure 2. It shows
that the spiritual-psychic emerges and ceases with the biological.
Thus, for the majority, the period of maximum activity and
responsibility in work, home and society is also the period when
the feeling of life as meaningful is also at its maximum. This leads
Bühler to conclude that a fulfilled life is 'to be there for something,
whether this be a human being, a thing, a work, an idea'. It also
underlines the problem that for many people life, in western
culture, is seen as having little meaning when the main external
tasks have been completed. This feeling is accentuated by the
way in which the old are treated and is a problem that all members

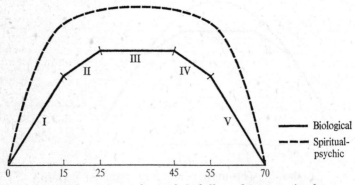

FIGURE 5 *An early peak is followed by sustained*
interest throughout the life-span

of the helping professions concerned with the elderly recognise.

However, Bühler found three other patterns of lesser frequency. These are illustrated in Figures 4, 5 and 6. Figure 4 represents those life-patterns where the spiritual culmination occurs during adolescence and youth and then sinks away during the period of high external involvement of adult life. Here, we could say, the idealism of youth has no staying power and gives ground under the pressure of life. But Figure 5 shows those less frequent cases where the concern with the meaning of existence does not fade, or is not allowed to fade, under the pressure of life, but continues as a basic concern throughout. Finally, in Figure 6, is illustrated the

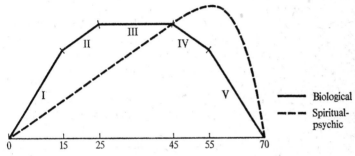

FIGURE 6   *The spiritual peak occurs only in the second transitional stage (Stage IV)*
(From J. Jacobi's *Way of Individuation*,
Hodder & Stoughton (1967))

emergence of the concern with the spiritual-psychic about the time when middle age occurs and then continues until death. Jung found that this latter pattern was common among the older clients he saw and encouraged it as a sound response to changes in role brought about by the decline of the biological capacities.

It is in studying and discussing Bühler's findings that some of the essential difficulties of talking and thinking about life-long development can be seen. It is probably easier to think about development in childhood and adolescence in largely empirical terms, because the adult researcher can distance himself better from these stages. This is less possible in studying the later stages and, in addition, development increasingly depends upon normative factors and upon factors which we have called 'the spiritual-psychic' or 'meaningfulness'. It was the recognition of this which led the existentialist Frankl (see p. 50 below) to specify 'the will to meaning' as the most potent human drive.

Nevertheless, Bühler has tried to be empirical and her work, in particular the finding that for the majority the spiritual-psychic culmination coincides with the most active period of work and family life, pinpoints one of the major problems of the life-cycle as a whole. This is the problem that the later stages, and particularly the last stage, of life are not often seen to be as significant in their own right as the earlier stages usually are. Some evidence on the varying attitudes that can be taken up towards the last stage of the life-cycle is now presented.

The Reichard study

Ageing and Personality: a study of eighty-seven older men by Reichard, Livsen, and Peterson (1962) is a report of a study carried out in the USA. The volunteer subjects were intensively interviewed, rated on various dimensions of personality and given psychological tests. They were men between the ages of 55 and 84, half of whom were retired and half still in either full- or part-time work.

The researchers did a multivariate analysis of 115 personality and other ratings of seventy of the subjects who could be clearly characterised as either well-adjusted or poorly adjusted. This analysis revealed five 'clusters' of subjects who may be regarded as illustrating five different strategies for adapting to 'old age'. Altogether forty-seven of these subjects could be clearly assigned to one or other of the five categories, leaving twenty-three who could not be so assigned.

The sample studied was small and the subjects came from a different culture to our own. Nevertheless, the research is interesting and makes a beginning in the study of adaptation to old age. The researchers tried to describe as well as they could the 'type' of individual represented by each of the five 'clusters' and brief descriptions of these 'types', necessarily very impressionistic, are given below (see Bromley, 1966).

Constructiveness This adaptation was found in fourteen of the subjects. It was significant that most had had a happy childhood, relatively little stress in adult life and a stable occupational history. This stability was reflected in their realistic and optimistic attitude towards retirement, old age and eventual death. They were characterised also by humour, tolerance, flexibility, self-awareness and reasonable self-sufficiency. As Bromley (1966, p. 106) says, 'His self-esteem is high and he can count on the support of people around him. He looks back on life with approval and few regrets and forward with anticipation to what is yet to come.'

Dependency This adaptation, found in six of the subjects, is characterised by passivity, submissiveness and dependence. The wife has become the dominant partner in the marital relationship and the husband accepts this in return for the emotional and material support that he needs. They are, however, well-adjusted and reasonably free of anxiety and neurotic symptoms. 'They have fairly good insight into their own personal qualities and actions, and manage to combine feelings of general satisfaction with the world (they are not anxious, disappointed or hostile) with tendencies towards unrealism, over-optimism and impracticability' (ibid., p. 107).

Defensiveness Seven subjects' adjustment could be described as defensive. These were men for whom retirement and inactivity represented a threat and for whom a busy life, avoiding retirement if possible, constituted a defence against a recognition of their old age and changed status. They retained the 'external' orientation characteristic of earlier life and rejected the need for reflection or self-examination (ibid., p. 108):

> They could see few advantages in old age, and were envious of young people even though they were satisfied with their own lives and achievements. They would come to terms with old age only when forced to do so. In the meantime, the prospect of old age and eventual death was ignored and avoided by keeping busy.

Self-blaming The type of adjustment of four of the subjects can be characterised as 'self-blaming'. These subjects were full of regret over the lives they had led, which were marked by lack of success in career and material terms. Their marriages had usually been unhappy with little warmth or affection. 'Their main feelings were those of regret, self-recrimination and depression. Death appeared not to worry them, since they saw it as a merciful release from a very unsatisfactory existence' (ibid., p. 110).

Hostility The adaptation of sixteen of the subjects was characterised as hostile. They lacked self-insight and reacted to the thought of becoming inactive and dependent by aggression, complaints and suspiciousness. They were unable to see anything positive in old age and therefore tried to remain busy and active for as long as possible. Their occupational history had been unstable and unsuccessful and as age increased so did anxieties and social maladaptations of various kinds. 'They envied young people and were hostile towards them. They could see nothing good in old age, they had not been reconciled to it and they were afraid of death' (ibid., p. 109).

It is interesting to note from a histogram of these findings (Figure 7) that a polarisation of attitudes on old age can be discerned. It is,

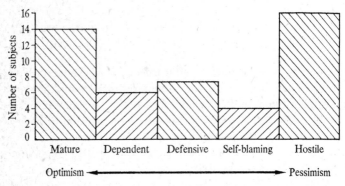

FIGURE 7 *A histogram illustrating the polarisation of attitudes and adaptation in old age in a sample of 47 subjects*

of course, improper to argue from this sample to the population at large, but the pattern is striking nevertheless. It gives some support to Erikson's assertion (see p. 16 below) that the conflict to be resolved towards the end of life is *Ego-Integrity* versus *Despair*. Figure 7 shows that for the sample studied nearly two-thirds are to be found at the extremes with the rest spread out between.

It was said at the beginning of this chapter that it was a reasonable assumption that emotional and intellectual maturation is a life-long process. We can go further now and say that it is not certain, in any individual case, what the final result of this process will be, because the ability and willingness of an individual to reflect on his experience and to integrate it is crucial. In addition, of course, as the Reichard study shows, the actual talents, opportunities, mishaps and successes tip the balance of an individual life in one direction or another. Erikson, however, the subject of our next section, argues for the notion of the life-cycle as purposive throughout. He puts forward a conflict theory, in which at successive stages one of two possible outcomes may ensue. As might be expected, the nature of the conflict at each stage is determined by the characteristic internal needs and external demands of that stage of the life-cycle.

Erikson's eight ages of man

Erik Erikson, a European who now lives in the USA, was trained as an analyst in Vienna, worked with H. A. Murray at Harvard and, after holding academic posts at Yale and Berkeley, is now Professor of Human Development at Harvard. He practised psychoanalysis, being particularly influenced by the ego-psychology movement within those of the analytic persuasion. The profound influence which anthropology has had upon him is reflected in his concern with the social roots of the ego. He is best known for his book *Childhood and Society* (1963) which first appeared in 1950 and from which the following ideas are taken.

On childhood, Erikson says (p. 16):

> Long childhood makes a technical and mental virtuoso out
> of man, but it also leaves a life-long residue of emotional
> immaturity in him. While tribes and nations, in many
> intuitive ways, use child training to the end of gaining their
> particular form of mature human identity, their unique version
> of integrity, they are beset by the irrational fears which stem
> from the very state of childhood which they exploited in their
> particular way.

While Erikson accepts the basic Freudian analysis into *id*, *ego* and *superego*, he concentrates on spelling out the process by which the particular *qualities of the ego* develop. In doing this, he emphasises the interaction between the organism and its environment as the most important causal factor. He concludes from his work that there are, in the course of life-long development, eight clearly discernible types of psycho-social conflict which call for resolution. Their successful resolution 'creates at every step ... an accruing sense of ego-strength' (p. 246). He presents his stages essentially in terms of 'a list of ego qualities which emerge from critical periods of development-criteria (identity is one) by which the individual demonstrates that his ego, at a given stage, is strong enough to integrate the time-table of the organism with the structure of social institutions' (ibid.).

The first stage: basic trust v. basic mistrust In the first year of life, the basic learning the infant has to achieve is the ability to trust its environment. Whether the ego develops with a basic trustfulness towards the world or not depends on this. In infancy, then, the pattern is laid down in the maternal care the infant gets. If this is characterised by sameness and continuity, then this leads to a sense of personal identity in later life which is rooted in 'a sense of being "all right", of being oneself'. As Erikson puts it (p. 249):

> There are few frustrations in either this or the following stages which the growing child cannot endure, if the frustration leads to the ever-renewed experience of greater sameness and stronger continuity of development, towards a final integration of the individual life-cycle with some meaningful wider belongingness.

Each of the needs of man, outlined in the eight stages, Erikson relates to a particular element of social organisation which acts to reinforce his infantile gains. In this case, he sees organised religion as the social expression of this need.

The second stage: autonomy v. shame and doubt In the second year of life, Erikson states that the child's greatest need is to experience and control a growing sense of autonomy; he needs a sense of being able to stand on his own feet. Nevertheless, he is inexperienced and has to learn painfully how to use his growing powers. The child's other need, therefore, is to be spared meaningless and arbitrary experiences of shame and doubt from excessive punishment visited on him for his unwise use of his decision-making powers. If he is handled at this stage with some understanding of these needs, then the seeds of his later autonomy are sown.

If he is punished a lot, however, the shame and doubt will be the preponderant feelings. Instead of learning to rely upon a gradually maturing decision-making process, the severely punished child doubts his own ability to function competently and independently. In later adult life, such a child becomes a person chronically in doubt and prone to feel ashamed. Erikson uses the notion of 'a favourable ratio' to explain a satisfactory outcome of each successive stage (p. 254):

This stage, therefore, becomes decisive for the ratio of love and hate, co-operation and wilfulness, freedom of self-expression and its suppression. From a sense of self-control without loss of self-esteem comes a lasting sense of goodwill and pride; from a sense of loss of self-control and of foreign over-control comes a lasting propensity of doubt and shame.

The third stage: initiative v. guilt Between the third and fifth years, Erikson believes that the basis of the later adult's capacity for initiative is laid. The outcome required from this stage is a favourable ratio of initiative over guilt. The capacity for initiative in the context of play (now possible through the growth of motor and mental abilities, and making possible competition, rivalry and co-operation) needs to be used. At the same time, the child's superego has been formed and is, at this stage, a rather primitive instrument. Equally, the parent stands by, ready to chastise or correct.

The child's first attempts at initiative (i.e. competing and co-operating) will lead to inevitable failures, and if they are punished severely, or, equally important, if they over-control or over-restrict themselves, then, instead of the satisfactions of initiative, the child will experience resignation and guilt. The later adult will then be prone to experience, in a variety of life-situations, guilt, acquiescence and feelings of unworthiness. Another possible outcome is where the child's internal over-control has been the striking feature of the period. 'The resulting self-righteousness ... can later be most intolerantly turned against others in the form of persistent moralistic surveillance, so that the prohibition rather than the guidance of initiative becomes the dominant endeavour' (p. 257).

The fourth stage: industry v. inferiority During what Freudians call the latency period, Erikson sees a preoccupation with the foundations of later productive life as the basic 'ego' problem. A satisfactory resolution of this period is a 'favourable ratio' of industry over inferiority. The child's life at this time is taken up with learning to handle tools, learning skills and the capacity to attend to, and be diligent in, systematic learning. Erikson's point is not only that the child is supposed to develop these skills, but *needs* them also.

This need is frustrated if he comes to feel inadequate and inferior through not being able to learn the skills or handle the necessary tools. If he feels he cannot match the skills of his peers, he may consider himself doomed to mediocrity or inadequacy. The empathetic teacher or parent will, following Erikson, realise that for each child there must emerge the feeling that there are roles he can fulfil in the wider society. In the language of self-theory (to be developed in the next chapter), an adult self-concept which includes the belief that one can cope and make a useful work-contribution must be a basic characteristic of the self-actualising person.

The fifth stage: identity v. role confusion At the end of childhood comes the beginning of youth and the onset of puberty. This stage is crucial to the development of the adult self-concept, for the task now is to relate together in a meaningful way a number of factors, viz. how others see one; how one sees oneself; what skills and abilities one possesses; and the role opportunities in society and their appropriateness to oneself. The need here is to link together past, present and future in a meaningful way. Erikson believes that doubts over sexual identity or occupational role are the big problems and can precipitate delinquent or psychotic behaviour.

Group membership of peer groups is one method used to resolve the conflict. 'For adolescents not only help one another temporarily through much discomfort by forming cliques and by stereotyping themselves, their ideals, and their enemies; they also perversely test each others' capacity to pledge fidelity.' Another method is identification. 'To help themselves together they temporarily over-identify, to the point of apparent complete loss of identity, with the heroes of cliques and crowds' (p. 262). The third method is projection (ibid.):

> To a considerable extent, adolescent love is an attempt to arrive at a definition of one's identity by projecting one's diffused ego image on another and by seeing it thus reflected or gradually clarified. This is why so much of young love is conversation.

By these methods, argues Erikson, modern youth seeks to meet its need to define its identity in an industrialised and urbanised world.

The sixth stage: intimacy v. isolation If the individual adolescent has emerged from the previous stage with a favourable ratio of identity over role confusion, he is now willing as a young adult to fuse his identity with another in the relationship of intimacy.

Intimacy is defined by Erikson as 'the capacity to commit oneself to concrete affiliations and partnerships and to develop the ethical strength to abide by such commitments, even though they may call for significant sacrifices and compromises' (p. 263).

On the other hand, if the sense of personal identity is not strong 'the solidarity of close affiliations, in orgasms and sexual unions, in close friendships and in physical combat, in the experiences of inspiration by teachers and of intuition from the recesses of the self' (p. 264), will be avoided because of a fear of ego loss and 'may lead to a deep sense of isolation and consequent self-absorption' (ibid.).

Erikson asserts that it is only at this stage that true genitality can develop 'for much of the sex life preceding these commitments is of the identity-searching kind, or is dominated by phallic or vaginal stirrings which make of sex life a kind of genital combat' (ibid.). He defines genitality in the following way (p. 266):

> mutuality of orgasm, with a loved partner of the other sex,
> with whom one is able and willing to share a mutual trust and
> with whom one is willing and able to regulate the cycles
> of work, procreation and recreation, so as to secure to the
> offspring, too, all the stages of a satisfactory development.

He adds that isolation need not be solitary. 'There are partnerships which amount to an isolation *à deux*, protecting both partners from the necessity to face the next critical development —that of generativity' (ibid.).

The seventh stage: generativity v. stagnation Erikson states that this is the central stage of adulthood. To resolve this conflict is the central need of the adult (p. 267):

> The fashionable insistence on dramatising the dependence of
> children on adults often blinds us to the dependence of the
> older generation on the younger one. Mature man needs to be
> needed and maturity needs guidance as well as encouragement
> from what has been produced and must be taken care of.

Although generativity is primarily the concern to establish and guide one's own offspring, it is often generalised into a need to be concerned with the next generation as such, and even more widely into the needs for productivity and creativity which are satisfied in the relationship with one's productive tasks as well as with one's progeny.

When the enrichment of the individual due to the satisfaction of this need fails altogether (ibid.):

> then regression to an obsessive need for pseudo-intimacy takes place, often with a pervading sense of stagnation and personal impoverishment. Individuals, then, often begin to indulge themselves as if they were their own—or one another's—one and only child; and where conditions favour it, early invalidism, physical or psychological, becomes the vehicle of self-concern.

The eighth stage: ego integrity v. despair In a book which is predominantly concerned with childhood, Erikson's observations of the eighth stage of the life-cycle are necessarily brief, but they are also illuminating. He begins (p. 268):

> Only in him who in some way has taken care of things and people and has adapted himself to the triumphs and disappointments adherent to being, the originator of others or the generator of products and ideas ... only in him may gradually ripen the fruit of these seven stages. I know no better word for it than ego integrity.

He lists the ego qualities of this stage: a growing assurance that one needs order and meaning in one's life; feeling that life as such is a worthwhile experience; an acceptance of one's own particular destiny and experience; a re-evaluation of one's own parents; a belief in the dignity of one's own life-style with a corresponding respect for those common in other cultures; an absence of fear of death because one sees this as the natural termination of one's life-cycle.

The failure to satisfy the need for ego-integrity leaves the individual in a state of despair, disgust and fear of death. The predominant feeling of despair is that one's life-cycle did not lead anywhere and that one will not get another chance to find a more meaningful way. This despair, however, may not break surface but be represented by a thousand little disgusts.

Erikson is finally concerned with bringing the life-cycle round into a full-circle by seeing the relationship between adult integrity and infantile trust. He sums this up epigrammatically, 'healthy children will not fear life if their elders have integrity enough not to fear death' (p. 269).

Summary

The case made out in this chapter is that we need to see human development in the context of the whole life-cycle, and the evidence from Bühler, the Reichard study and Erikson has been brought forward to support this view.

Bühler's significance is in underlining the importance of the spiritual-psychic dimension. Nevertheless, it can hardly be argued that it is indispensable to human existence since, as she shows in Figure 2, the biological ground-plan does suffice to illustrate the existence of some individuals. However, I take her main point to be that there is in the human organism the phenomenon of self-consciousness and the use of this ability in taking up a view towards the goals of one's strivings is a specifically human characteristic; and the periods of life in which this is salient enables her to make distinctions between different life-cycles (Figures 3-6) to which most thoughtful observers of human life will give their assent.

The Reichard study, slender though its empirical basis is, helps us to bring into focus the forms of adaptation possible in the later stages of life. The *constructive* strategy illustrates the possibility of a satisfying and adaptive response to old age. This is important evidence in an age when the *active adult life* is taken by many as the paradigm of human existence and when old age is stereotyped as either embarrassing or ridiculous. However, it is clear that a continuity of development is apparent and the better one's adaptation to childhood and adulthood, the better one's adaptation to old age, though Reichard's evidence does show that a constructive adaptation to the last stages is not incompatible with periods of neurotic disturbance at earlier ones.

Of the writers studied, Erikson gives us the most thorough developmental picture. His value is in seeing development as truly psycho-social at all stages. He relates together the developing inner needs at any given stage with the corresponding external demands and pressures. He sees development as emerging out of this tension with a possibility for a positive or negative outcome always present. For our particular purpose, Erikson's emphasis on the identity crisis of adolescence is particularly relevant. The individual's need to discover who he is and what his potentialities are relates to our concern in the next chapter with the self-concept and points towards the possibility of continual revisions of this identity, which is what is meant by the concept of self-actualisation.

2

Towards self-actualisation

In chapter 1, a case was made for putting individual development within a life-long context in order to give a rationale for social work intervention. And reference was made to a number of models of the 'life-cycle' which make plausible the view that development at each stage of life is purposive. The object of the present chapter is to look at the dynamics of this development more closely. This part of the book may not seem to have much to do with social work, but it is a necessary foundation for later more practical sections.

The self-concept

A number of contemporary writers use, more or less synonym-ously, the terms 'self', 'self-structure', or 'self-concept'. They refer to the fact that, as a result of socialisation, an individual comes to take a partly conscious, partly unconscious view of his own totality. This structure consists of a set of attitudes towards, or beliefs about, one's own needs, goals, abilities, feelings, values, prejudices, self-characteristics, and methods of relating to other people. (The extent to which these different attitudes are integrated with one another is the extent to which the individual is mentally 'adjusted'.) This structure, or self-view, operates at a number of levels; it acts as a filter through which experience is mediated; it acts as a framework by means of which meaning can be given to experience; it also acts as a guide to decisions, choices and selections of possible alternatives.

Once the self-concept is formed, it is very resistant to change and comes to constitute the basis on which future psychological development is likely to take place. According to Carl Rogers (1965) who has articulated this idea most clearly, it becomes the channel through which the individual's emotional and behavioural potential is expressed. Alongside the self-concept, which is learned from one's family and within a particular culture, there is also a 'genetic blueprint' of special abilities and personality-type and a biological tendency towards the realisation of the blueprint. As the self-concept is developed more from teaching and by introjection of parental assessments of one's abilities than from self-discovery, it is often out of line with the 'genetic blueprint', thus creating disharmony between the biological and psychological strivings of the organism.

Rogers (1965), Argyris (1965), Maslow (1954) and others use the term 'self-actualisation' to describe the tendency of the human organism to develop in ways that are consistent with the existing 'self-structure' but Rogers has given the most detailed account of the phenomenology of this process.

Symbolisation, or the capacity to verbalise our experiences and behaviour, is the crucial factor. Take, for example, someone who believes himself to be a mild, non-aggressive person. From time to time, perhaps when watching the aggressive behaviour of others, he will reassure himself with the thought of his own non-aggressiveness. This belief about himself will also mean he is not able to be aware of his own aggressive feelings when they occur. For experiences that cannot be symbolised in accordance with the self-structure represent threats to the integrity of that structure against which the individual must defend himself. Such a person, therefore, will be always in a state of actual or potential tension. He is maladjusted. And the solution to this lies in his developing or being helped to develop a wider and more realistic self-concept which will permit a wider range of experiences to be symbolised without distortion.

Preserving the self-concept

Rogers's emphasis on the role of symbolisation is seen in the following quotation (1965, p. 503):

> As experiences occur in the life of the individual, they are either (a) *symbolised*, perceived and organised into some relationship to the self, (b) ignored because there is no perceived relationship to the self-structure, (c) denied

symbolisation or given a distorted *symbolisation* because the experience is inconsistent with the structure of the self.

On point (b), we can accept that, at all times, stimuli, sensations or pieces of behaviour are not symbolised or even perceived, because of their irrelevance to our temporary or permanent concerns. But, perhaps, a trivial example will illustrate points (a) and (c).

Let us imagine a person who holds as part of his self-concept, the belief that he is clumsy with his hands. When such a person fails to mend something, he is well able to symbolise and perceive this experience, seeing this as a confirmation of his self-structure, i.e. 'I'm no good with my hands at all'. But a successful attempt at mending something has to be symbolised in a distorted fashion, e.g. 'I don't know how I managed it. I'm sure I couldn't do it again'. This illustrates the fact that the self-concept has to be defended, in some instances, even against positive experiences. For the important factor is the continued preservation of the self-concept in broadly the same form.

Developing his argument further, Rogers says 'behaviour may, in some instances, be brought about by organic experiences and needs which have not been symbolised. Such behaviour may be inconsistent with the structure of the self, but in such instances, the behaviour is not "owned" by the individual' (p. 509). For illustration of this point, we return to our earlier example of the supposedly mild, non-aggressive person. If he gives vent to an angry outburst or shows very aggressive behaviour towards somebody, he is likely to feel very uneasy. He will seek, therefore, to allay this uneasiness or tension by asserting to himself or others 'I'm not really like that' or 'I don't know what came over me'. In this way the self-concept is preserved.

We are familiar with the idea of defensiveness from the work of Freud and his many successors. Argyris has attempted to bring together the self-theorists and the psychoanalysts at this point. He says that the experiences of anxiety, frustration, conflict and failure are the principal occasions on which the self feels threatened and hence tries to take defensive action. As we noted earlier, the self-concept includes self-image, perceived needs, valued goals and abilities. Threats to different aspects of the self-concept seem to have a distinctive quality; hence, threats to valued needs we call frustration; threats to desired goals, failure; fear of loss of self-image, anxiety; competition between different aspects of the self-concept, conflict. Of course, it is the precise nature of an individual's self-concept which will determine the precise occasions when he will feel anxious, frustrated, conflicted or a sense of failure.

Argyris lists sixteen different defence-mechanisms which we may use to defend ourselves from threatening situations and goes on to describe the effect of the excessive use of defence-mechanisms (1965, p. 37):

> For example, let us say that Supervisor A feels threatened
> because he 'knows' his boss does not think that he (Supervisor
> A) is doing a good job. Let us assume he defends his
> self-concept by placing the blame on the boss. This will not in
> any way stop the boss from feeling the way he does about
> Supervisor A. Soon the Supervisor will have to justify his
> defensive reactions to himself. He may do this by saying
> the boss is 'out to get him'. Each of these defences is a
> distortion which in turn will require further justification
> and further defence. After some time, Supervisor A has built
> up deep layers of defence, all of which will have to be
> uncovered if he is to understand the cause.

Transcending the self-concept

We have so far stressed the fact that the self-structure is highly resistant to change, and also that incongruence between self-concept and experience leads to maladjustment. Furthermore, a maladjusted person cannot possibly actualise his potentialities, for thoughts, feelings and actions which truly express inherent potentialities are rejected if they should be inconsistent with the learned self-concept.

However, one of the major assertions of the self-theorists is that, given certain conditions, an individual can change the self so that it becomes congruent with whatever is causing the 'threat' to it. The discovery and use of these conditions becomes vital if individuals are to move towards more satisfactory forms of the self, rather than simply defending inadequate self-concepts.

Rogers (1967) has set out in his therapeutic encounters to provide an atmosphere of unconditional positive regard; an atmosphere, that is, in which his client clearly understands that he is valued and respected by the therapist, whatever his feelings and behaviour at any particular time. The willingness of an outside person to accept his (the client's) less desirable feelings and be-haviours encourages him to examine the said feelings and be-haviours instead of reacting defensively to them.

This kind of experience produces a type of person who
(a) has a respect for and values all manifestations of himself.
(b) has a consciousness of virtually all there is to know about him-self.
(c) has a flexibility and openness to experience.
It must be emphasised that a new basis for values arises from within the individual rather than being imposed from outside.

Clearly, therapy for all is not possible. But it seems to me that the importance of Rogers's methods of client-centred therapy lies in showing that the inertia exerted by one's existing self-concept is not insuperable, and that in certain types of relationships, individuals can develop self-concepts that make self-actualisation really possible.

We shall look, in the next chapter, at a variety of ways in which individuals can help themselves, or be helped, to 'transcend the existing self-concept', where they need to do so. Here it is sufficient to stress that self-actualisation only involves transcending the self-concept when that self-concept is incongruent with the experiences and potentialities of an individual. But where an individual is able to value, appreciate, enjoy, respect and respond to all his various needs and experiences, then development will be in accordance with his self-view. On the other hand, where the self-concept is narrow and inappropriate to an individual's needs, it will tend to channel that life along a narrow, unsuitable, and often self-stultifying channel, and such a structure has to be modified in order that a more suitable matrix for development may be constructed.

The judgment as to whether an individual's self-concept is inadequate, narrow and unsatisfactory is not an arbitrary one. The human organism signals in a number of ways the poor fit between self-view and potentiality. Neurotic symptoms, behaviour disorders, social inadequacy, feelings of boredom and often physical illness are the objective evidence of the poor fit between self-concept and organismic needs. On the other hand, creativity, tolerance, and a number of other positive factors have come to be regarded by the self-theorists as evidence of a good fit. These are the self-actualising people who are the subject of the next section.

A. H. Maslow's 'self-actualising people'

The most penetrating psychological analysis of motivation published in recent years is that by A. H. Maslow (1954). He argues that the basic human needs are organised into a hierarchy of relative prepotency. The physiological needs (e.g. for food, water, warmth and sleep) occupy the bottom level in the hierarchy. If they are ungratified, all other needs are virtually non-existent. But when well gratified, the next level in the hierarchy comes into play. This level consists of the 'safety needs' which are satisfied for the normal adult when he finds himself in a peaceful, stable, smoothly-running society. But these needs become dominant again in natural and political emergencies. When physiological and safety needs are regularly being gratified, a yet higher level of needs becomes potent, the 'belongingness and love' needs. Following their gratification, the needs for esteem, respect and status come into play. Finally, if all the previous four levels are regularly gratified, the need to actualise oneself emerges.

Maslow explains self-actualisation by saying (1954, p. 91):

> Even if all these needs [of the first four levels] are satisfied,
> we may still often (if not always) expect that a new discontent
> and restlessness will soon develop, unless the individual is doing
> what he is fitted for. A musician must make music, an artist
> must paint, and a poet must write, if he is ultimately to be
> at peace with himself. What a man *can* be, he *must*
> be. This need we may call self-actualisation.

The need to self-actualise is not only found in those with artistic abilities. In others, it may take 'cognitive' forms. The human organism if not cognitively involved falls into boredom, self-dislike and general depression of bodily function. For such conditions, Maslow advocates 'cognitive therapy', for example, taking up an intellectually more demanding job or immersing oneself in something more worthy of one.

To give his work a sound empirical basis, Maslow needed a group of individuals who could be identified as self-actualising people and from a study of whom the characteristics of optimal human functioning could be inferred. His negative criterion for inclusion in the group was an absence of neurosis, psychopathic personality or psychosis; and, positively, a use of their talents and capacities and high-achievement. His final group numbered 45 and included acquaintances, friends and public and historical figures.

The outcome of the study may best be summarised by listing the fifteen characteristics which constitute his overall impression of these people.

(1) They have a more than usually efficient perception of reality and more comfortable relations with it. That is, they perceive others more accurately and they tolerate uncertainty better.

(2) They show acceptance of self and others. That is, they have relatively little guilt, shame or anxiety. They are not defensive about their shortcomings.

(3) They live spontaneously. But they are not unconventional for its own sake; they will suppress unconventionality for the sake of others' feelings.

(4) They are not ego-centred. Rather they are oriented to solving problems outside themselves. They often have a mission in life.

(5) They do not avoid privacy; they actually seek it. They can detach themselves and look at things objectively.

(6) They are autonomous. That is, they are able to be relatively independent of the general social milieu in which they live.

(7) They continually derive ecstasy, inspiration and strength from the basic and ordinary experiences of life.

(8) They often have 'peak experiences'. They are quasi-mystical experiences involving the feeling of being outside time and space. Following these experiences they have the conviction that something extremely valuable and important has happened.

(9) The term *Gemeinschaftsgefühl* best describes their feelings for mankind. That is, they have a feeling of identification, sympathy and affection for mankind, although they are realistic about the shortcomings of the species.

(10) Their inter-personal relationships can be very deep but usually with a few rather than with many individuals. They are capable of expressing hostility, but such hostility is reactive rather than chronic.

(11) They have a democratic character structure. That is, they can learn from, and relate to, people irrespective of class, education, race and religion.

(12) They feel it important to differentiate between means and ends. And, while they rarely lose sight of the end within the means, they can enjoy the means without impatience.

(13) They are characterised by a sense of humour which is philosophical and non-hostile.

(14) They are creative in the sense that one can be a creative carpenter or clerk. This creativity appears in their everyday life as the expression of a personality which is perceptive, spontaneous, expressive, childlike and without fear of the unknown.

(15) They are not well-adjusted in the naïve sense of approving of, and being identified with, their culture. They can relate satisfactorily to their culture in various ways but they maintain, in a profound way, a certain inner detachment from the culture in which they are immersed.

Maslow emphasises that these people are not perfect. They have many ordinary human failings and can, on occasion, be ruthless, can alienate others, and can be indifferent to others' needs. But they are experiencing a more integrated form of functioning than most people. Also, they do seem to be solving in a more imaginative way the perennial conflict between our individual needs and the social and organisational demands that are made upon us.

The importance of Maslow's analysis of self-actualising people is that it helps to operationalise the notion of self-actualisation. For the danger of references to human fulfilment is that they may end up as rather confused and cloudy descriptions of fictional heroes. This point will be taken up again in chapter 4 in a critical assessment of the concept of 'self-actualisation'. Also, as the concept of 'need' in social work is so confused, the reader might like to consider whether Maslow's hierarchy of needs has not something to offer social work in this regard. We will take this up later (chapter 5).

Carl Rogers on 'the fully functioning person'

We find in Rogers's writings a similar analysis to that put forward by Maslow. Rogers's term is 'the fully functioning person' (1967). He applies this term to people who, through therapy, obtain a better fit between self-concept and organismic potentiality. The general pattern he sees is as follows:

(1) Openness to experience. This is opposite to defensiveness. It is an absence of distortion of those feelings that tend to 'threaten' the self-concept. It also means that ability to experience more completely feelings of courage, tenderness and awe.

(2) Increasingly existential living. By this is meant an ability to live

creatively and spontaneously; an ability to dispense with rigid personality configurations; an absence of 'obsessional orderliness'; it means a maximum of adaptability.

(3) An increasing trust in one's organism. Rogers says of this (1967, p. 189):

> I find that increasingly such individuals are able to trust their total organismic reaction to a new situation because they discover to an ever-increasing degree that if they are open to their experience doing what 'feels right' proves to be a competent and trustworthy guide to behaviour which is truly satisfying.

(4) Experiential freedom. The 'defensively organised' person reacts to experiences with predictable defensive strategies. There is no freedom in this. But the fully functioning person feels free and experiences the freedom of actually choosing and moving in new directions.

(5) Creativity. He is the person most likely to adapt and survive under changing environmental conditions. He is able to make sound adjustments to old as well as new conditions.

At the conclusion of his essay on the fully functioning person, Rogers sums up his attitude towards the phenomenon that he has been describing (pp. 195-6):

> adjectives such as happy, contented, blissful, enjoyable do not seem quite appropriate to any general description of this process.... But the adjectives which seem more generally fitting are adjectives such as enriching, exciting, rewarding, challenging, meaningful. This process of the good life is not, I am convinced, a life for the faint-hearted. It involves the stretching and growing of becoming more and more of one's potentialities.

C. G. Jung and 'individuation'

It is a main argument of this book that a human desire for self-realisation and a distinguishable personality-type called the 'self-actualising person' exists. Scientists in widely different fields of endeavour have produced, quite independently of each other, broadly similar ideas. A notable contribution has been made by Carl Gustav Jung (1875-1961), the Swiss founder of analytical psychology.

Jung called the desire for wholeness, *individuation*. Jolande Jacobi in her book *The Way of Individuation* (1967, p. 13) has explained the term as follows: 'a possibility of development immanent in everyone ... that culminates in rounding out the individual into a psychic whole'. But there are two kinds of individuation. First, the natural process, occurring more or less autonomously and without the participation of consciousness. And, second, the artificial process aided by psychoanalysis, developed by definite methods and consciously experienced.

In both forms, the same power is at work, striving for maturation and self-realisation. But the two forms are as different as a wild fruit and a highly cultivated one. For example, 'there are people who, entirely by themselves, without using special methods or needing any guidance, let alone the help of analysis, win to that wholeness and wisdom which are the fruits of a life consciously experienced and assimilated, all its battles fought' (ibid., p. 17). But equally, there exist in many cultures, forms of discipline which facilitate the process of individuation.

Jung did not present a pattern of motivation as complex as Maslow's, but he did recognise the logical chronology of development throughout human life. In the first half of life the aim of individuation is the adaptation of the individual to outer reality—work, the family and society. Neuroses in younger people are to be seen as indications of failure of adaptation in one or all of these areas. In the second half of life (i.e. from middle age on), the need for self-realisation or individuation assumes its greatest importance. If the need is recognised by the individual and appropriate methods to assist the process are taken up, then life can be given fresh meanings and the characteristic sense of loss in middle age, of which depression is a symptom, can be overcome. Jung also taught that individuation includes a psychic preparation for death.

The course of individuation, leading to wholeness, is not linear; it is more like a spiral. And in analyses in the first half of life, the preoccupation is with the *shadow*, Jung's term for the repressed disagreeable aspects of oneself; in the second half, preoccupation is with the *anima/animus*, the term for the unconscious contrasexual characteristics. Beyond these figures lie others, essential to development, but consciousness is not broad enough to accommodate them until the *shadow* and the *animus/anima* have been accepted and assimilated.

Jung believed that the process of individuation had a goal, which he called the *Self*, and which he took to be a synthesis of all psychic aspects, both conscious and unconscious. He taught that there was a special sort of relationship between the Ego and the Self in the individuated person. The Ego becomes subordinated to the Self in such people. This is not an experience which diminishes one's sense of autonomy but rather one has a greater sense of inner certainty, security and purposeful direction.

Jung was plainly fascinated by 'individuated persons' and remarks, in particular, their self-acceptance, to which Maslow also refers. Jung says, 'they came to themselves, they could accept themselves; and thus were reconciled to adverse circumstances and events' (1958b, p. 81).

His work lacks the systematic approach of Maslow's, but a number of statements descriptive of the 'individuated person' can be culled from Jung's writings:

(a) They live their own lives, rather than seeking mainly to adapt.
(b) Being individuated is a form of human dignity, which is not simply based on recognition by the mass.
(c) They strike a balance between being true to themselves and being a member of the collective.
(d) They are not outstandingly intelligent nor necessarily talented in any other way. Anyone can with the right determination achieve relative wholeness.
(e) Despite their capacity for isolation, they are not recluses; their relationship to their fellows becomes more tolerant, deeper, more responsible and more understanding. They can open themselves up to others, since they do not fear that the other will take possession of them, or that they will lose themselves in the other.
(f) The 'individuated person' does not suffer from the characteristics of individuality, namely, ego-centredness and eccentricity. He recognises his obligations and yet remains a whole person.

I believe that the reader will find substantial agreement between Jung's descriptions of the 'individuated person' and Maslow's description of 'self-actualising people'. There is however one striking difference, which is Jung's absence of reference to the 'peak experiences' which Maslow has referred to.

Maslow asserted that peak-experiences occur in a variety of circumstances such as 'in ... the parental experience, the mystic or oceanic, or nature experience, the aesthetic perception, the creative moment, the therapeutic or intellectual insight, the orgasmic experience, and certain forms of athletic fulfilment' (1968, p. 78). And about such experiences, individuals use such words as wonder, awe, unity, perfection, timelessness and meaningfulness.

Jung's ambivalence towards religion and his fears of becoming involved in mysticism led him to play down this aspect of experience. But in his autobiography, *Memory, Dreams and Reflections* (Jaffé, ed., 1963), published posthumously, there is a chapter entitled 'Visions', which indicates both the recurrence of such 'peak experiences' in Jung's own life and the profound impression they made upon him. He, in fact, regarded mystical experiences as experiences of archetypes.

Wilhelm Reich and loosening the character armour

Our discussion so far has been conducted in terms of motivation-theory, viz. the self-actualising tendency, and individuation. Reich, however, speaks more directly of an actual pulsating life-force. He refers to 'the orgonotic streamings' which can, for example, be experienced as a result of breathing exercises properly carried out. It seems to me that Reich's discovery has a great deal to offer our present discussion. And equally that the formulations of Maslow, Rogers and Jung are pertinent to the case that Reich tried to make out.

Reich (1969) was very concerned with the psychologically deformed person whom he called a character-neurotic, whose neurosis showed itself not in symptoms so much as in a stunted personality. He coined the term *character-armour* to describe the rigidity of behaviour which such a person developed as a means of dealing with his central conflicts. Reich proceeded in therapy with the intention of loosening the client's character-armour.

He held the view that character-armour would be expressed not only behaviourally but also in terms of muscular tension. He introduced *doing* or *activity* into therapy. He worked at deepening the breathing of the client and breaking down the muscular armour. When these techniques led to the release of emotions as they usually did, the client was encouraged to assist their release by hitting, kicking or yelling.

A neurosis, on this view, is equivalent to a system of blockages which prevent the free flow of feelings throughout the body. The muscular rigidity binds up anxiety and sexual feelings. Mental resistance or repression is expressed physically as physical tension. Muscular rigidity in different parts of the body has its own special significance. For example, rigidity in the eye muscles often signifies buried suspicion or repressed crying, telling the therapist the nature of the client's early relationships. Or again, tensions in the neck are very common; stimulation of the muscles of the throat and neck often releases anger and sorrow which have been choked back in infancy. The avowed aim of bio-energetic therapy is to overcome these blockages and to restore the free flow of feelings through the body.

When the individual overcomes the main tensions in his body by massage and postural movements, he experiences his body in a new way. He also functions well sexually and finds an ability to surrender fully to other experiences, e.g. work, music, painting, a dramatic performance, and a close relationship with another person. When the *armour* is destroyed, full plasma mobility is re-established and the individual experiences the full capacity of pulsation. Reich regarded as a very significant index of mental health the capacity for involuntary physical mobility. The orgasm is one example of this. And Reich asserted that in a fully experienced orgasm, one not limited by reason of the muscular armour, the organism actually gives itself over to the orgonotic streamings, the actual pulsating life force. But the orgasm is only a special case of a more general phenomenon, and in support of this view, Reich and his successors have shown that a number of breathing procedures, for example, can, if properly carried out, lead to experiences of involuntary pulsating muscular mobility of a more general kind.

The significance of the Reichian work for my overall case is that he recognised that the average person is alienated from the vital springs of life that nourish individual human existence. In the language of the earlier sections, the self-concept of the individual is too narrow to express his total feelings, needs, aspirations and creative intuitions. Many of these are, in fact, locked out of the conscious mind and the muscular rigidity referred to is the physical expression of these resistances. On the other hand, when individuals are able to break down these stultifying mechanisms, unresolved conflicts do break surface; but when with therapeutic help, these have been worked through, the individual feels a new source of dynamism and begins to operate at more integrated levels of functioning. This more satisfactory level of functioning, we would expect to show considerable similarities to that of the self-actualising people already discussed.

The contribution of Andreas Angyal

Another writer whose work is germane to our theme is Angyal, psychiatrist and researcher into human functioning. Angyal put forward a conflict theory. In order to make sense of human behaviour and experience, he asserted the existence of two basic drives, viz. the drive towards *autonomy* and the drive towards *homonomy*.

Of the former he says (1941, pp. 131-2):

> man strives basically to assert and expand his self-determination. He is an autonomous being, a self-governing entity that asserts itself actively instead of reacting passively like a physical body to the impacts of the surrounding world. This tendency expresses itself in spontaneity, self-assertiveness, striving for freedom and mastery.

However, autonomy operates within the social and physical environment. Angyal expressed the interplay of autonomy and heteronomy (environment) in terms of the following function.

$$\left(\frac{a}{h}\right)_1 \ll\longrightarrow \left(\frac{a}{h}\right)_2$$

By this he means, the ratio of autonomy to heteronomy tends to increase over time. The tendency of the organism in its productive activity (i.e. building, creating, and changing the environment) and in its growth leads to an increased control of the environment. Even the phenomenon of regression did not, he believed, disprove this, for our tendency is always to move forward. In sum (ibid., p. 132):

> life is an autonomous dynamic event which takes place between the organism and the environment. Life processes do not merely tend to preserve life but to transcend the momentary *status quo* of the organism, expanding itself continuously and imposing its autonomous determination upon an ever-increasing realm of events.

In contention with the drive towards autonomy is the *drive towards homonomy*, i.e. the drive to find a place in something which is greater than oneself; whether this be family, clan, nation,

a cause, an ideology or an ordered universe. Much of human behaviour can be seen as an expression of this tendency; it is
expressed through common modes of dress and food preparation,
through conformity to the norms of one's group and in the religious
attitude. In Angyal's view, the study of history is an expression of
this tendency.

There is a need, on the one hand, for mastery, independence and
dominance of others, and, on the other, for sharing, participation
and union. A successful compromise is needed in which there is self-
surrender without dependency and possessiveness and self-reliance
without lack of respect for the norms of the group and the rights
of others.

Two key concepts in Angyal's work are *differentiation* followed
by *integration*. Angyal, both as researcher and psychiatrist, was
convinced that the successive stages of differentiation followed by
integration were fundamental to human growth, learning skills and
also self-actualisation. They can be observed in a child learning to
use his hands and fingers, a person learning to type efficiently, or an
individual moving towards maturity (ibid., p. 273):

> The evolution of any whole takes place in successive stages of
> differentiation and the re-imbedding of the differentiated parts
> into the whole. Differentiation always includes a kind of
> disequilibrium because it is a stage that leads beyond the
> present status of the whole. The process of differentiation is
> normally followed by a process of assimilation or re-imbedding
> whereby the whole itself changes to some extent.

In terms of a learning curve, the plateau is the stage of differentiation, and the rising part of the curve is the change in behaviour,
i.e. improved efficiency.

The value of this work, it seems to me, is to emphasise the
homonomous tendencies as well as the autonomous. Also the
reference to self-actualisation as step-by-step process of differentiation followed by integration, is an important idea which helps to
make our notion of the self-actualising process more realistic.

Schachtel and world-openness

E. G. Schachtel, biologist, psychologist and researcher into human
perception, has emphasised self-actualisation (1959). He says 'the

movement of life is towards increasingly greater mobility, relative separateness of the organisms from their immediate environment and individuation'. There is a conflict—forces also pull the organism back—but, in most healthy individuals, the forces making for growth are more impressive than the fears of embeddedness, or the fears of venturing into a new, unknown way of life.

Schachtel criticises Freud for overlooking the forces making for growth in the individual, while playing up man's tendency to fly from reality. Also, as a student of evolutionary theory, he makes the point that Freud has confused phylogenesis (evolution) with ontogenesis (psychological motivation). Freud argues as if man's development were largely phylogenetic, i.e. through the pressure of environment; but, in fact, man's development is largely and typically ontogenetical, i.e. it is the enjoyment of realising or exercising potentiality. In his own experimental work, Schachtel was profoundly impressed by the eagerness of the growing child for a wide variety of sensory stimulation and for the pleasure and fulfilment to be found in mastering an ever-expanding reality.

Schachtel's basic concept is 'world-openness'. He means by this man's drive to relate to the world. He refers to the way in which objects and persons in the world are experienced in their own right. What distinguishes man also from other mammals is his need to pose the questions, 'Who are you?', 'Who am I?', 'What is the world?', 'What is to be my relation to the world?' Even the highest mammals are not open to the world in quite this way. Even in infancy and childhood, this attitude to the world is visible, but it may become buried and forgotten by the time he is an adult.

He has shown that the conflict (referred to above) between world-openness and embeddedness leaves its traces in the whole psychology of the individual. 'Every human act bears the traces of the emergence from embeddedness, even though neither the actor nor others who perceive the act may be aware of this.'

The perceptual counterpart of world-openness is called by Schachtel 'allocentric perception'. And in so far as the individual has retained and developed his capacity for world-openness, he will perceive allocentrically, that is, objectively. But, where world-openness has become buried, the individual perceives only the socially-accepted 'reality' around him.

Schachtel's research into perceptual differences led him to propose the following three stages in the development of an individual's capacity for perception:

(1) *Autocentric perception*   The infant's perceptions are pre-eminently subjective. His perceptions reflect his own needs and feelings, and there is little capacity to perceive objective reality.

(2) *Allocentric perception*   Increasingly as the organism grows, there develops a capacity for object-centred perception. This is marked by a profound interest in the object for its own sake; an ability to allow the object or person to make its unique impact upon one; a capacity to attend fully to an object. This capacity is unique to the human species.

(3) *Secondary autocentric perception*   A third stage inevitably develops, as a result of socialisation, and may come to overshadow the other two stages. There is a tendency to see 'reality', as defined by one's group, society or culture. The 'reality' which is 'seen' here is 'a socially accepted reality'. This is an aspect of regression and a form of stultification of human potentiality.

Schachtel uses the term 'the allocentric attitude', which symbolises for him the approach to life of the complete and well-functioning individual. It seems to resemble certain aspects of the 'self-actualising person' as already defined. The 'allocentric' individual has a capacity for profound interest in the object, complete openness and receptivity, totality and affirmativeness of interest. He is not a defensive person. And, one might speculate, if he should attain at any time complete allocentric perception, this is what in Maslow's terms would be called a peak experience.

The work of Kurt Goldstein

There is also evidence for self-actualisation from neurological research. Goldstein, a neurologist, whose book *The Organism* was published in English for the first time in 1939, made a special study of the behaviour of brain-damaged patients. These patients' disordered processes gave Goldstein deeper insight into normal mental and behavioural functioning.

Goldstein was a man of many original views, including disagreement with the widely accepted mind-body dichotomy, and scepticism about the value of animal experiments. On motivation, his views are interesting. He regarded the 'self' and the organism as virtually the same, hence self-actualisation, for him, means the biological push to realise one's potentialities. Unlike other psychologists who postulate many drives, Goldstein believed that there is only one, viz. the self-actualising drive. Although much behaviour gives the impression of stemming from independently existing drives, such behaviours are simply instrumental prerequisites of the self-actualisation of the organism.

Somewhat like Angyal and Schachtel, Goldstein offers us a conflict theory. The drive to self-actualisation comes up against the forces of the environment; shock and anxiety are generated in this encounter; however, the anxiety has to be borne and overcome for the sake of the actualisation of one's own nature. Crucial to the ability to cope with anxiety is seeing a single experience within a larger context and retaining the capacity for decision and choice. Courage is really the ability to bear anxiety. 'Individuals differ as to how much anxiety they can bear. For a patient with brain injury, the amount is very low, for a child it is greater, and for the creative individual it is greatest' (1939, p. 306).

In Goldstein's considerable experience, the brain-injured person is found to be completely helpless when facing an anxiety-situation. He experiences anxiety as *catastrophic anxiety*, the fear of coming to an end, of being overwhelmed, or disintegrating. At such a point, the life-enhancing process of self-actualisation ceases, and the life-maintaining processes come into play whose aim is to enable the person to survive, through an enormous limitation of his world which reduces his human existence to the most simple forms.

However, 'the tendency towards actualisation is primal' and the self-actualisation tendency will lead to the fulfilment of the genetic blueprint, unless normal social support is lacking, or physical danger is present.

Goldstein's analysis is relevant to our subject and it raises many questions for our consideration; the central one being the role of anxiety in holding back self-actualisation. As we noted, Goldstein remarked on the individual differences in anxiety-tolerance. There are the brain-damaged patients and the creative individuals who represent the extreme ends of the spectrum. But in between are the numerous neurotic and defensive persons, whose self-actualisation is limited through failure to develop a positive attitude towards anxiety.

G. W. Allport and creative becoming

For the final contribution to this survey of the dynamics of self-actualisation, we look to G. W. Allport, an academic psychologist with a strong interest in personality theory. The sense of the self ('proprium') he regards as being made up of the following:

Bodily sense: A certain body and certain sensations are recognised as one's own.

Self-identity: The sense of being a particular separate person with one's own name and remembered experiences.

Ego-enhancement: The capacity for pride, humiliation, self-esteem and narcissism.

Ego-extension: An individual comes to call certain objects 'mine'. They become matters of importance to him.

Rational agent: The capacity to find solutions, make appropriate adjustments and to plan effectively.

Self-image: This is the self-concept or self-structure. It includes a self as one is (actual self) and a self as one wishes to be (ideal self).

Propriate striving: It is the possession of long-range goals which is the specifically human form of motivation.

The knower: This is the part of the self that cognises the rest of the self. It is the 'I' which relates to the 'Me'.

It is Allport's notion of propriate striving which is his special contribution. He sees the course of individual growth as depending, in the first instance, on the *chance* factors of inheritance and environment. Then there are the *opportunistic* factors, such as the opportunity to learn certain skills. But the final factor in growth is propriate striving, the course of life we choose as a means of achieving a special life-long objective or satisfying a dominant interest. It confers unity on personality; it creates more tension not less; the pursuit of a dominant objective distinguishes human from animal, the adult from the child, and the healthy personality from the sick.

Moral development, which is part of the development of the self-image, shifts gradually from a 'must' essence to an 'ought' essence. This is a development from external to internal constraints. However (1955, p. 74):

> Conscience may be arrested in its development. Plenty of people, adult in years, have not successfully effected these transformations. They suffer from infantile guilt, from unresolved conflicts with early authority figures. But the pathology of conscience does not alter the rules governing its transformations in the normal course of becoming.

Allport believed that there was a process within the individual towards maturity, called 'creative becoming' or 'the normal course of becoming'. Central to this process are the broad intentional dispositions of the individual, which are always few in number. The more basic needs, attitudes, skills and so on are simply the raw materials out of which the 'proprium' builds its edifices or, alternatively, they are the means to the organism's important ends.

Summary

In this chapter, our concern has been the dynamics of the self-actualisation process.

The self-concept is central and fosters self-actualisation if it is consistent with the inherited biological tendencies. But if out of line with them, conflict is generated against which the individual must defend himself. Rogers has explored the conditions under which an inadequate self-concept may be transcended and a more realistic one developed. Naturally, development of potential is more spontaneous when an individual's self-concept is open to experience and congruent with it.

The people who are continuing to develop themselves have been studied by Maslow, who has worked out a detailed life-long motivation theory. His value is in helping us to be realistic about self-actualising people. Rogers and Jung have, in their own separate terminologies, made out similar cases, and contributed additional insights. Reich's controversial theories explore the actual physical expression of an individual's alienation from the sources of energy essential to continual development.

In the latter part of the chapter, a small selection of thinkers, from four separate fields, viz. psychiatry, biology, neurology and psychology, were introduced as being relevant to this theme.

Angyal has explored the way in which the need for mastery is reconciled with the need to belong to an entity larger than oneself. And like Maslow, he emphasises the step-by-step nature of individual development. Schachtel transposes our theme into a different key in showing that even perception reflects the state of self-development within an individual.

The value of introducing Goldstein into this context seemed to me his emphasis on the role of anxiety in self-development and also the fact that the life-maintaining processes should not be ignored. Finally, Allport supplies the important ingredient of the role of values and of life-goals in optimal development. As we noted, his analysis of the 'self' is most precise.

In sum, this chapter presents the main theories regarding the life-long process of self-actualisation. It is intended in a later chapter to look at them critically. The other chapters will be largely concerned with the problems of facilitating this process, over which these authorities have shown so much unanimity despite differences of terminology. For our purpose is the very practical one of teasing out the implications of these ideas for actual, everyday, social work.

3
Methods of fostering self-actualisation

In the previous chapter (p. 23) in discussing the self-concept and its crucial role in the development of the individual, we said we would go on to consider ways in which individuals can help themselves, or be helped, to transcend their existing self-concept where they need to do so. It was pointed out that self-actualisation only involves transcending the existing self-concept when it is incongruent with the experiences and potentialities of an individual, and that the organism signals in a number of ways the 'poor fit' between self-concept and potentiality. We now turn to the practical methods of fostering this sort of development in individuals and groups.

The social worker as counsellor

There is a current interest among social workers in the *counselling* aspects of social work. By this we mean an interest in the extent to which a social worker can use an actual interview with a client to explore with that client here-and-now feelings, problems and behaviour so that self-insight into these conditions is achieved. At the same time, there is concern about the slowness of this process and a need for reassurance that this apparently slow process can build up, little by little, into eventually observable improvement in the functioning and adaptation of the client.

It is clear that the amount of counselling in casework varies among individual social workers and from interview to interview. Peter Leonard (1966, p. 37) describes something of the conflict in his description of the initial interview:

Very often the social worker views the initial interview as one in which he explores the ground with the client in order to see whether the social work agency can help the person being interviewed. In other words, he sees the role of the interviewee not as that of actual client, but of potential client or applicant for the service which the social work agency provides. The interviewee, on the other hand, may see her own role as actual client and she, therefore, expects that her problems will be taken up and worked on immediately.

Regardless of whether the client's problems referred to here are material or emotional or both, this statement about an aspect of casework does reveal a difference in time-perspective between agent and client. The client expects help here and now, the agent, however, is collecting information on the basis of which *future* action may be taken.

This difference in time-perspective is believed by some social workers to have pervaded the whole relationship. John Coop, senior probation officer, takes up the following position (private communication to the author, 22 December 1972):

> The casework approach has previously dominated probation service practice. Casework is largely *past* and *future* oriented. It is concerned with the history of the client and his future rehabilitation. But there has been, to a large extent, a neglect of the present situation and what could be done in the here and now. There has been little emphasis on taking the opportunity to understand and help the client to work through present feelings and attitudes. Now counselling is coming into its own and an officer will counsel more and use the present encounter more constructively.

That this process has gone some way is illustrated by the following description of casework with the violent client in the probation service. A. R. Sabine describes such work as having five elements (lecture, Hollinwood, Oldham, 20 May 1973):

> (a) Helping the client to realise the situations in which he finds himself which act as 'triggers' for his violent behaviour and discussing ways in which he can avoid them in the future.
> (b) Allowing the client to express his aggressive feelings to the social worker as a release-mechanism.

(c) Helping the client towards greater self-knowledge which may eventually have a limiting effect on his aggressive behaviour.

(d) The necessity of introducing 'controls' on the client from time to time, when they become necessary.

(e) Identifying the client's main personal and social problems so that efforts can be made to alleviate them.

It is clear that this approach is predominantly a counselling one, unavoidable, perhaps, with the violent client, where it has long been recognised that the root of the behaviour-disorder derives from a failure in his integration and adaptation.

The reader is referred to Table 1 (p. 44) for an outline of a basic counselling model. This pattern may be repeated in part or in full on a number of occasions, if the agent is working with the client over a considerable period of time. The reader is advised to study this 'model' before reading on.

It will be clear that this is not an argument for a return to the old and classic psychodynamic approach to casework which was largely based on drawing a distinction between the 'presenting problem' and the 'underlying and real problem' behind it. Neither is it an argument that the social worker should become a psychotherapist, though some really sick clients will always need to be referred to such resources. Counselling is about the here and now, about discussing current feelings, values, attitudes and reactions as a basis for moving forward. It is not based on reductionism, i.e. the belief that *only* by bringing the client's experiences in infancy, childhood and adolescence to light can current problems be solved.

In any case, humanistic psychology, of which the self-actualisation theories form a part, takes a relativistic view of the concept 'personality problem'. As Maslow (1968, p. 6) says:

The classical approach to personality problems considers them to be problems in an undesirable sense. Struggle, conflict, guilt, bad conscience, anxiety, frustration, tension, shame, self-punishment, feelings of inferiority or unworthiness —they all cause psychic pain, they disturb efficiency of performance, and they are uncontrollable. They are therefore automatically regarded as sick and undesirable and they get 'cured' away as soon as possible. But all of these symptoms are found also in healthy people or in people who are growing towards health. Supposing you *should* feel guilty and don't? Supposing you have attained a nice stabilisation of forces and you *are* adjusted? Perhaps adjustment and stabilisation while good because it cuts your pain, is also bad because development towards a higher ideal ceases?

Maslow underlines his relativistic view, 'In a word if you tell me you have a personality problem, I am not certain until I know you better whether to say "Good" or "I'm sorry". It depends on the reasons. And these, it seems, may be bad reasons, or they may be good reasons' (ibid., p. 7).

Counselling, in the sense in which it is used here, starts from the view that we must create a climate in which the client can hear the voice of his own 'inner core' (cf. Jung's concept 'the self', p. 29 above), and also the voices of his other impulses and can begin to listen to this inner dialogue and, with the worker's help, bring the dialogue to a conclusion (Maslow, 1968, p. 191. My italics):

> This inner dialogue, even though it is biologically based and 'instinctoid', is weak in certain senses rather than strong. It is easily overcome, suppressed or repressed. It may even be killed off permanently. Humans no longer have instincts in the animal sense, powerful, unmistakable, inner voices which tell them unequivocally what to do, when, where and how and with whom. All we have left are instinct-remnants. And, furthermore, these are weak, subtle and delicate, very easily drowned out by learning, by cultural expectations, by fear, by disapproval, etc. They are *hard* to know, rather than easy. *Authentic selfhood can be defined in part as being able to hear these impulse-voices within oneself*, i.e. to know what one really wants or doesn't want, what one is fit for and what one is not fit for, etc. It appears that there are wide individual differences in the strength of these impulse-voices.

In the previous paragraph, I spoke about 'bringing the dialogue to a conclusion'. The reader will understand that this is not a final conclusion that is referred to. All the counsellor can do is to create within the client a respect for his own 'authentic self' and foster in him, not by teaching but by creating the conditions in which he can learn, a desire to continue the dialogue. For the process of self-actualisation, as all authorities agree, is life-long.

TABLE I Basic counselling model

Stages	Subsidiary stages	Counsellor's role
1 Establishing rapport		Putting client at ease and creating an open channel of communication.
2 Ventilation		Listening to the client and encouraging him to talk.
3 Understanding the problem		Helping the client to come to as full an understanding of his problem as possible.
4 Decision-making	A Is the client really *aware* of the nature of his problems? (See Stage 3 above.) B What are the various possible solutions? And what are their advantages/disadvantages? C What is the best solution for this client and what are its implications if adopted? D How can the chosen solution best be put into operation?	To keep the *process* of decision-making in mind. Helping the client to make *his* own decision but ensuring that he has worked through all these stages.
5 Terminating the interview		To summarise the progress made. And, if appropriate, to go over any plans made for implementing decisions made. To arrange future interviews.

Note: The interview need not necessarily go through all five stages. It can end, as the arrows show, after Stage 2 or Stage 3. Or during Stage 4.

This table is taken from the author's *Basic Counselling* [1973].

In the next section we look at Carl Rogers's views on his own methods of fostering self-development in the client.

The client-centred approach of Carl Rogers

One of the classic formulations of counselling has been outlined by Carl Rogers in a number of books and has come to be called the 'client-centred' approach. Rogers's views have been in circulation since the early 1940s but they are now more relevant than ever since the 'humanistic psychology' movement, which gives a central place to 'self-actualisation', has only emerged, as a conscious force, within the last decade.

Central to Rogers's practice are the two related notions of 'conditional positive regard' and 'conditions of worth'. They can be briefly explained as follows. If a child, or even a young person learning an occupational role, has only *some* but *not all* his actions, thoughts and feelings approved of, and supported by, the significant people in his life, then his self-concept when formed will be the product of this *conditional positive regard* and will itself be based on *conditions of worth*. This is to say, the individual can give himself only conditional approval. He disapproves of himself when he experiences recurrences of the behaviour, thoughts and feelings that earned the disapproval of his parents, teachers and mentors. Conditions of worth when present logically imply defensiveness, i.e. when that person has some small inkling or clue that some unworthy behaviour or feeling is likely to occur then defences are activated. Rogers emphasises the defence mechanisms of denial and distortion and that these, like all other defence mechanisms, have the effect of keeping the threatening experience at arm's length and preserving the individual from the humiliating experience of self-disapproval.

In Rogers's view both *conditions of worth* and *defences* are crippling because they can lead to a rejection of thoughts, feelings and actions which express inherent potentialities of the individual. These experiences when faced and worked on become the raw material out of which future growth will come. But if the individual continues to reject them he is left in a static state of incongruence between self-concept and experience. In brief, once conditions of worth exist, it is impossible fully to actualise one's potentialities. One has lost out on some of one's own genetic birthright.

As mentioned in the previous chapter (see p. 22 above), Rogers believed, therefore, that the most useful thing he could do for his client was to provide an atmosphere of *unconditional positive regard*. By this he meant that the client is valued and respected as a person without qualification; his behaviour, feelings and thoughts are accepted and supported, even though they may be disagreeable to the agent.

The method of client-centred counselling is non-directive in that objective interpretations of the client's feelings and behaviour, persuasion, giving advice, and the exertion of subtle forms of pressure are avoided. As Rogers says (1965, p. 24):

> the individual has a sufficient capacity to deal constructively
> with all those aspects of his life which can potentially
> come into conscious awareness. This means the creation
> of an interpersonal situation in which material may
> come into the client's awareness, and a meaningful
> demonstration of the counsellor's acceptance of the client
> as a person who is competent to direct himself.

He suggests that the only scientific way one can become convinced of the soundness of this proposition is to treat it as a hypothesis which has to be tested out on each new client and patiently followed. Patience is vital because (ibid.):

> If the counsellor feels, in the middle of an interview, that
> this client may not have the capacity for reorganising
> himself, and shifts to the hypothesis that the counsellor must
> bear a considerable responsibility for this reorganisation,
> he confuses the client, and defeats himself. He has shut
> himself off from proving or disproving either hypothesis.
> This confused eclecticism, which has been prevalent
> in psychotherapy, has blocked scientific progress in the field.

This method of counselling has sometimes been characterised as a *laissez-faire* approach in which the counsellor does nothing apart from reflecting back in a more precise way the client's confused attempts at describing his own experiences. What Rogers emphasises, however, is empathy (ibid., p. 29):

> It is the counsellor's function to assume, in so far as he is able,
> the internal frame of reference of the client, to perceive
> the world as the client sees it, to perceive the client himself
> as he is seen by himself, to lay aside all perceptions from

46

the external frame or reference while doing so, and to communicate something of this empathic understanding to the client.

Or, as it is put more vividly by Raskin (unpublished, quoted by Rogers, ibid.):

> At this level, counsellor participation becomes an active experiencing with the client of the feelings to which he gives expression; the counsellor makes a maximum effort to get under the skin of the person with whom he is communicating; he tries to get within and to live the attitudes expressed instead of observing them; to catch every nuance of their changing nature; in a word, to absorb himself completely in the attitudes of the other. And in struggling to do this, there is simply no room for any other type of counsellor activity or attitude; if he is attempting to live the attitudes of the other, he cannot be diagnosing them, he cannot be thinking of making the process go faster.

Rogers's conviction that the self-concept is crucial to the whole process is expressed as follows (1946, pp. 420-1. My italics):

> We have come to recognise that if we can provide understanding of *the way the client seems to himself at this moment, he can do the rest.* The therapist must lay aside his preoccupation with diagnosis and his diagnostic shrewdness, must discard his tendency to make professional evaluations, must cease his endeavours to formulate an accurate prognosis, must give up the temptation subtly to guide the individual, and must concentrate on one purpose only; that of providing deep understanding and acceptance of *the attitudes consciously held at this moment by the client as* he explores step by step into the dangerous areas which he has been denying to consciousness.

In other words, if one can help the client to grasp the present self-concept he holds, one releases in the client constructive forces towards a reorganised self-concept which will be less at variance with the inner and outer reality of the client's life (Rogers, 1965, pp. 48-9):

> To me it appears that only as the [counsellor] is completely

willing that *any* outcome, *any* direction, may be chosen—
only then does he realise the vital strength of the capacity
and potentiality of the individual for constructive action.
It is as he is willing for death to be the choice, that life is
chosen; for neuroticism to be the choice, that a healthy
normality is chosen. The more completely he acts upon his
central hypothesis, the more convincing is the evidence
that the hypothesis is correct.

The characteristics of a helping relationship

In his book (1967, pp. 39-57), Rogers has given a number of concise
guidelines to an effectively helpful counselling relationship.

(1) If the counsellor can be sensitive to, and acceptant of, his own
feelings, especially during the counselling interaction, then the
likelihood is that he can help the other person to be aware of his
own feelings as they occur.

(2) Effective counselling is facilitated if the counsellor can discard
the need for an impersonal 'professional' relationship and can
allow himself to feel positive emotions towards the client. This
means setting aside the fears that out of such emotions excessive
demands may ensue that we feel we cannot meet or that our trust
may turn out to be misplaced, leading to disappointments.

(3) The effective counsellor needs to be sensitive to the depression,
fear, despondency or anger of the client, yet strong enough not to be
overwhelmed or taken over by these feelings.

(4) The most effective counsellors do not wish to make the client
dependent on them or to turn them into carbon-copies of themselves. They allow the client to develop a personality which is
quite distinct and in line with their own needs.

(5) If the counsellor enters fully into the client's world, he will
lose the wish to evaluate it as he is caught up in the desire to
understand it as fully as possible. The communication of this
empathic understanding to the client turns out to be extremely
helpful to him.

(6) If the counsellor can accept only some, and not all, aspects of
the client's self as he reveals it to him, then it turns out that the
client cannot or does not grow in those areas of himself which the
counsellor, because of his own fears, met with resistance or silently
or openly disapproved of.

(7) If the counsellor can create a relationship in which the client

feels safe through not being pressured by the counsellor, he will set to work himself, of his own volition, on the feelings and conflicts that he feels threatening within himself.

(8) The meaning and value which the client sets on his experiences is in the end something which is up to him. Hence the counsellor by refraining from acting as an external source of meaning and value sets the client free to be a self-responsible person.

(9) If the counsellor is deeply convinced of the potentiality of people generally and tries to regard each client as a person in the process of becoming, then this will contribute to the possibility that unrealised potentiality will be released and made real.

(10) The degree to which the counsellor can be helpful to the client in the ways described depends on the extent to which he has himself learned to listen to and reflect on his own feelings, intuitions and opinions.

Logotherapy as an approach to counselling

Counselling theories and methods come in many forms and the reader would be wrong to think that the non-directive method associated with Rogers alone constitutes sound counselling. Victor Frankl, the exponent of logotherapy uses a more directive style. After reading the present section, the reader might consider whether Frankl's method or the previous one is more suited to his own personality, attitudes and the kind of client he habitually sees; or, indeed, whether he ought to search the literature on counselling for himself for a relevant approach (see further reading below). Rogers has pointed out that a counselling method cannot be based satisfactorily on a set of superficial attitudes. It is only effective if it is in tune with the individual counsellor's deep-seated attitudes and he adds that some 'professional workers may find it very difficult to learn or to practice a client-centred form of [counselling]' (1965, p. 21).

Frankl is the author of many books, most of which have now been translated into English. The most notable of these include *The Doctor and the Soul* (1969a) and *The Will to Meaning* (1969b). In this exposition, I shall be drawing mainly on the latter. Frankl coined the term 'logotherapy' (which means literally healing through meaning) because, in his view, existential analysis, associated as it is with many quite different practitioners, such as Binswanger, Rollo May, R. D. Laing and others, including Frankl, has become too confused a term to describe what he, Frankl, is trying to do.

Frankl makes three basic assumptions about human existence. First, the freedom of the will: by this he does not mean to imply that human life is unconditioned. This is plainly false, because we are conditioned by physical, psychological, social and cultural factors. Freedom of the will, in Frankl's sense, means man's freedom as to the attitude he takes up towards the conditions that confront him. Second, the will to meaning: in Frankl's picture of human motivation the drive to find a meaning for one's existence is fundamental. He has also called this the need for self-transcendence. Third, the meaning of life: being human is being directed to something other than oneself (cf. Bühler, p. 6 above). There is, however, no such thing as a universal meaning of life, but only the unique meanings for unique individuals in unique situations.

He sees a significant role for the counsellor who is not a psychotherapist or a psychiatrist, because of the prevalence in modern life of the 'existential vacuum' (a sense of meaninglessness and emptiness). He concludes as a result of his own clinical experience that about one in five of all people who come to him in distress are not suffering from psychogenic or somatogenic mental disturbances, but from what he calls 'noögenic neuroses'. Some of these originate in spiritual problems, in moral conflicts or in the conflict between true conscience and mere super-ego. Mostly, however, they stem either from the frustration of the will to meaning (existential frustration) or from the presence of an existential vacuum.

For the sufferer from a noögenic neurosis, Frankl adopts the role of a helper to the client as he tries to discover a meaning in his life. He asserts that he cannot give meanings but he can help the client to discover meanings for himself. However, he has a lot to say about *values*, which are the key to finding meaning. A value is a value because it is one way in which an individual finds meaning in his life and thus avoids the existential vacuum.

Frankl distinguishes three types of values. First, creative values: when an individual creates something, for example, a work of art, a job well done, a child reared, a book written, he gives something to the world and also finds a meaning in his life. Second, experiential values: when a person has satisfying encounters, experiences and human relationships, he finds meaning in his life. Third, attitudinal values: when a person takes a courageous stand towards a fate or a predicament which he cannot change, he gives meaning to his life. On this last category, Frankl (1969b, p. 70) states:

> This is why life never ceases to hold a meaning, for even a person who is deprived of both creative and experiential values is still challenged by a meaning to fulfil, that is, by the meaning inherent in the right (or upright) way of suffering.

As was said earlier, Frankl's method of counselling is more directive than Rogers's, but essentially persuasive not coercive. With the client whose problem is to find a meaning which will give point to his existence, a transcript of a Frankl interview takes on the appearance of a Socratic dialogue, in which he communicates his superior wisdom, based on his knowledge as to where the values are likely to be found which will give a meaning to the life of this unique individual. It seems to me that the types of client who will benefit most from this approach are the younger client, the more intelligent and those who either for reasons of training or personality want an authoritative style from the counsellor rather than the sort of co-partnership required by Rogers's method.

The following brief extract from an interview between Frankl and a student with a noögenic neurosis gives some idea of this method (ibid., p. 91-3).

> He suffered from a recurrent dream in which this experience of life's total meaninglessness manifested itself. In these dreams, he would find himself among people whom he urgently asked for a solution of his problem, for liberation from this situation. He would beg them to free him from the anxiety that his life was in vain. But they would just continue to enjoy their lives, to enjoy meals, to enjoy sunshine, or whatever life had to offer them. When he had described this dream to me, the following dialogue took place:
>
> Frankl: That is to say, they enjoy life in a wholly unreflective manner?
>
> Patient: Right! While I am crippled by my doubts as to the meaning of my life.
>
> Frankl: And what do you try to do to help yourself?
>
> Patient: Sometimes it brings me relief to hear and play music. After all, Bach, Mozart, and Haydn were deeply religious personalities, and when enjoying music, I

enjoy the fact that at least its creators have been granted the good fortune to arrive at a full conviction that there is a deeper or even ultimate meaning to human existence.

Frankl: So, even if you do not believe in such a meaning yourself, you believe at least in the great believers?

Patient: You are right, Doctor.

Frankl: Well, isn't it the mission of the great leaders in religion and ethics to mediate between values and meanings on the one hand, and man on the other? Man is thus given a chance to receive out of the hands of a genius of humanness, be it Moses or Jesus, Muhammad or Buddha—he is given the chance to receive from them what he is not in each instance able to obtain by himself. You see, in the field of science our intelligence might do. With respect to our beliefs, however, we must sometimes rely on and trust in other people greater than ourselves, and adopt their visions. In his search for an ultimate meaning of being, man is basically dependent on emotional rather than merely intellectual resources, as we know; in other words, he must *trust* in an ultimate meaning of being. What is more, however, this trust must be mediated by his trust in some*one*, as we now see. But now let me ask you a question: What if music touches you down to the depth of your being and moves you to tears, as is certainly the case at some moments, isn't it?—do you then, too, doubt the meaning of your life, or do you not even question it at these moments?

Patient: This problem then does not come to my mind at all.

Frankl: Right. But isn't it conceivable that precisely at such moments, when you are in immediate touch with ultimate beauty, you have found the meaning of life, found it on emotional grounds without having sought for it on intellectual ones? At such moments we do not ask ourselves whether life has a meaning or not; but if we did, we could not but shout out of the depth of our existence a triumphant 'yes' to being. Life, we would feel,

would be worth-while even if only lived for the
sake of this unique experience.

It is clear from other extracts in the same book that the level
of explanation used by Frankl varies depending on the kind of
client he is confronted with and on the nature of their life-situation.
However, the overall attitude remains the same. It is that life can
be lived if there are values which an individual can find that give
meaning to his particular situation. And Frankl takes upon himself
the very active role of helping the client to look in the particular
direction where he is likely to find the values that will give him
the meaning he needs. His approach is particularly relevant to those
individuals who are caught up in what he calls the tragic triad,
namely, pain, guilt and death. These are common human experiences which are there to be understood; as Frankl would say, there
is attitudinal value in them for the individual. All social workers
who deal with clients in extreme situations will find something of
importance in what Frankl says about the tragic triad (ibid.,
pp. 73-5), even if one feels that his counselling method would be
inappropriate to one's own kind of situation.

Summary

So far we have concentrated on the dyadic encounter between
agent and client as a locus within which self-actualisation can be
fostered. First, we considered Rogers's method of creating trust,
safety and security so that the individual is able to examine those
aspects of himself which have been too painful to consider or
which he has distorted or denied. Second, the method of Frankl
which concentrates on building up the values of the client. Despite
the difference in terminology, his work relates to the self-concept
for he is concerned with fostering new ways of regarding oneself,
one's experience and one's situation.

Counselling, in its many forms, is appropriate for people who are
in a state of temporary mental disequilibrium and who want some
support while they are in the process of taking over control of
their own self and situation again. The common theme running
through the varieties of counselling theory is that this support
should be offered in such a way that the individual should be able
to achieve a greater feeling of autonomy not only in his present
crisis but will also, in future situations, be able to apply his present
learning so that support from outside is not necessary. This aim

Rogers, Frankl and others are, in their different ways, trying to achieve.

Group experiences as a means of fostering self-actualisation

The current vogue for, and use of, groups in personal development has developed from a number of sources. On the one hand, there has been work in social psychology (e.g. Lewin, 1952 and Asch, 1955, 1956) which has demonstrated the remarkable effectiveness of group situations in influencing individual behaviour. Lewin, in particular, demonstrated the superiority of the group over the typical dyadic situation in which the professional agent meets and talks with a client.

On the other, there has been the work of Wilhelm Reich (1969) on his concept 'character armour' (Shaw, 1972, p. 146):

> He made it clear that the neurotic personality could deal with its central conflicts by developing a certain rigidity of behaviour rather than by manifesting symptoms. Reich proceeded in therapy with the intention of loosening the client's 'character armour'. This he would do by concentrating on the behaviour of the client, e.g. his silence, his submissiveness, his complaints, or his tendency to provoke the analyst. Reich's aim was to try to arouse the client's interest in his own character traits in order to be able ultimately to explore analytically their origin and meaning. He aimed, therefore, to make the client self-conscious of his own behaviour; to confront him with a trait until he saw it as a harmful symptom and wanted to be rid of it. So, a submissive client, for example, when made fully aware of his submissiveness, tended to react with the aggression that the submissiveness had been designed to protect him from. Thus, the hidden conflicts which the character traits were designed to cover come to light and can be explored and, hopefully, dissolved. Out of this insight into the importance of character armour, a whole 'technology' has developed of sensitivity training, of T-groups and process groups—all situations, broadly, in which individuals can be made aware of their defensive character traits and of their function in the psychic economy.

Experiential groups, as we may call them, have been associated over the last couple of decades with the National Training Laboratories in Bethel, Maine, USA, with the Tavistock Institute of Human Relations in London and with the Esalen Institute, California, USA. It is essential, however, to point out that there are wide differences in orientation and technique associated with, for example, the work of Bion, Rice and Rogers. Perhaps all would agree over what experiential groups are not. As Aronson (1972, pp. 237-8) puts it:

> Typically it is not a therapy group—that is, it is not designed to cure mental illness; indeed, people with serious emotional problems are discouraged from attending. It is not a seminar —that is, it is not a group in which members communicate facts and abstract concepts about the world. It is not a group in which the leader is a traditional teacher, who tries to impart knowledge by lecturing to the members as though they were an audience. Neither is it a committee that performs tasks or solves problems that have originated outside the group itself. A T-Group experience is educational—but educational in a way that is different from what we are accustomed to. It is different both in the *content* of the material that is learned and in the *process* by which the learning takes place.

It will be recognised by the reader that a social worker meeting a group of clients is not in the classical T-group situation. These clients may be adolescents with behaviour problems, adult addicts, discharged patients or prisoners, mothers of multi-problem families, prospective foster parents and so on. What we are interested in spelling out here is the extent to which such groups can, in addition to achieving their own purposes of instructing, fostering adaptation and changing behaviour, also foster self-actualisation. (In chapter 5, however, groups which foster behavioural change are considered separately.)

The role of the group leader/trainer

In describing this role, a list of specific behavioural characteristics will be given, as in the section (on p. 48 above) on the helping relationship in dyadic situations.

(1) The leader has no specific goal for the group and sincerely wants it to develop its own direction. This attitude is compatible even with the fact that a learning group may have some quite

specific goals. There is considerable evidence now that quite specific learning goals can be reached by non-directive methods (see e.g. Belbin, 1969).

(2) He or she wants to be a participant like the other group members. One is responsible to the group but does not feel that one carries the sole responsibility for ensuring that the experience turns out to be worthwhile.

(3) The trainer tries to be present in the group as a whole person, that is, to interact with the group both emotionally and cognitively.

(4) He or she tries to create an atmosphere in which people feel both safe and free to be aggressive, or caring, or self-disclosing, in short, to be genuinely themselves.

(5) The effective group trainer accepts the group exactly as it is, even if they want to intellectualise the situation, or escape into discussion of trivial matters, or to mask their feelings. He is also prepared to let the individual members decide the extent to which they are willing to participate and in what way.

(6) He feels that the best contribution he can make to the group is to try to understand exactly what people are communicating to the group and to feed this understanding back to them. When he feels it necessary to confront an individual, he tries to base his remarks on their specific behaviour in the group and describes this behaviour and its effect on him rather than making evaluations.

(7) The trainer tries to be aware of his own feelings, fantasies and intuitions about the group and its members. He will express these to the group when he thinks they will facilitate the process of self-discovery.

(8) Some effective leaders make interpretative comments on the group process, others feel that such comments are usually more effective when they are voiced by participants.

(9) The trainer has a responsibility to be therapeutic or protecting towards individuals whose behaviour becomes disturbed or who are being hurt too much. However, the other participants ought to be given the chance to see this need and do something about it. Only if they don't will he feel it absolutely necessary to intervene himself.

(10) Some effective leaders use exercises or 'games' to break down rigidity or strangeness in a group or to move the group process into a new dimension.

These principles are taken, in the main, from *Encounter Groups* by Carl Rogers (1971, chapter 3). He, in particular, uses groups to help people to grow, whereas other supporters of groups are concerned with other issues, for example, helping people to work through feelings they have about authority.

Does group experience help individuals to grow?

The evidence for this falls into two different categories. There is the anecdotal evidence available through the expressed comments of individuals after a group experience. As one of Rogers's group members said (Rogers, 1969, p. 58, quoted in Aronson, 1972, p. 258):

> I am more open, spontaneous. I express myself more freely.
> I am more religious in my own way. I am more confident.
> My relations with my family, friends and co-workers are more
> honest and I express my likes and dislikes and true feelings
> more openly. I admit ignorance more readily. I am more
> cheerful. I want to help others more.

On the other hand, the experience for participants is sometimes transitory and at best a highlight on which one looks back with a certain amount of nostalgia.

There is also data of a much more rigorous kind. Eliot Aronson, a noted social psychologist, has this to say about the published data on the effects of T-group experience (1972, pp. 260-1):

> Most of the research done on T-groups lacks the control
> and precision of the laboratory experiment.... It remains
> difficult to be certain what causes what. At the same time,
> after surveying the research literature, I am compelled to
> draw the conclusion, albeit tentatively, that important
> changes do take place in T-groups, and that these changes are
> demonstrable beyond the individual's own self-report. In several
> studies, for example, it has been shown that other people
> outside of the T-group can see changes in participants that are
> consistent with the stated goals of the T-group and with the
> individual's own self-report.

In chapter 2 we noted among Maslow's characteristics of self-actualising people, the relative absence of racial prejudice among them. He said: 'they can learn from, and relate to, people irrespective of class, education, race and religion'. We would expect, therefore, that if T-groups foster the growth of an individual and make him self-actualising, then individuals should be less racially prejudiced after such an experience than they were before it. When Rubin (1967, pp. 29-50) devised an experiment to test this hypothesis he obtained precisely this result. Aronson (1972, pp. 261-2) summarises these findings briefly:

> Rubin simply administered a test designed to measure ethnic prejudice to a large group of people. Half of those people then went through a T-group experience. He then remeasured the ethnic prejudice of all of the individuals. Those who had gone through the T-group showed a sharp reduction in ethnic prejudice; those who had not gone through the T-group showed no sizeable change.

We also noted when considering Maslow's views that self-acceptance, tolerance of others and insightfulness came first on his list of the characteristics of self-actualising people. Dunnette and Campbell's research (1968, pp. 73-104) into the effects of group experience on industrial managers tests out the growth of these characteristics and others of specific importance to the managerial role. Again, Aronson's summary (1972, p. 261) of this research must carry considerable weight:

> An industrial organisation allowed a few of its managers to participate in a T-group. Several weeks later, the back-home colleagues of those individuals were asked if they had noticed any changes in their on-the-job behaviour. As a control the same respondents were also asked to note any changes in the on-the-job behaviour of managers who had not been in a T-group. By and large, the data showed a tendency for managers who had participated in T-groups to be viewed by their associates as having changed more than managers who had not. Specifically, the T-groupers were seen to be more sensitive; to have more communication skills and more leadership skills; to be more considerate of others, more relaxed, and more insightful; and so on. These data suggest that the effects are not simply a matter of self-deception on the part of the participants; they indicate that real changes occur that can be perceived by other people. These findings are encouraging, but not perfect.

Life-situations as opportunities for growth

So far, in this chapter, in considering situations in which individuals grow by self-discovery and self-reorganisation, we have concentrated on 'artificial' situations, viz. the professional agent-client
interview or the group of clients meeting with a worker in an
agency or institutional setting. However, increasing attention is
now being paid to events arising spontaneously in an individual's
life, for example, illness or crises within a marital relationship,
during which, if support can be given, self-understanding can grow
and the experience can become the opportunity for considerable
personal growth.

It was Freud who first drew attention to the fact that a neurosis
can be a 'gain' to an individual. He distinguished between Primary
and Secondary gain. Primary gain, for Freud, meant the intra-
psychic or internal gains, i.e. instead of anxiety and conflict, one
now has certain painful, but more straightforward symptoms; for
example, obsessional or hysterical characteristics. Secondary gain
meant the advantages that can be extracted from the fact of
having a neurosis; for example, by the scope the illness gives one
to manipulate or influence others.

Thomas Szasz (1961) and Peter Lomas (1965) have criticised this
distinction because it relegates the interpersonal and social gains to
the secondary role, but they do accept the general concept of 'gain'.
As Lomas says (ibid., p. 156):

> In our culture there is a defined role, that of being ill. . . . If
> any family member cannot by ordinary means gain or
> maintain the position of power that he wishes for or feels to
> be his right, the adoption of a sick role is a possible
> alternative method of attaining his desired goal. All he has
> to do is to convince the family that he has some avoidable
> incapacity and having attained this strategic position to launch a
> counter-attack on those in power. Such a move is similar to
> the deliberate sacrifice of a piece in chess, and is, of course,
> no guarantee of success.

He adds that the struggle for ascendancy can be waged in a
different way; the strategy might be to retain or gain power by
making the other person sick.

The realisation today is that considerations like these apply beyond neuroses to psychoses and physical illness. Lomas continues (pp. 160-1):

> Sickness in an individual usually carries a potential for growth and the manifest symptoms contain, in disturbed form, elements of the real nature of the person which have previously remained in repression. When this occurs the function of the therapist is to 'hold' his patient in much the same way as a mother 'holds' her baby, extending the use of this term to include more than the immediate physical handling.... With the help of these ideas, it becomes possible to conceive the sick role as a temporary asylum, necessary in terms of crisis and growth, by means of which the ordinary commitments are avoided and the energy saved can be utilised for the purposes of reorganisation.

Goldstein (see p. 36 above) is also associated with this view.

This positive view of illness opens up a role for individuals in helping professions, for example, nurses, social workers and counsellors, which is expressed by Lomas as 'holding' or supporting and by Wolff (1965, p. 51) who describes the role in a more complex way:

> In order to help patients to live without having to express their unconscious fantasies from time to time in a variety of psychosomatic diseases they need to be made aware of their repressed fantasies, impulses and conflicts and be helped *to find their true self and live a life appropriate to it.* This demands that they no longer deny certain aspects of their personality and are prepared if necessary to follow their true self even if this should bring them into conflict with some of the more conventional and restrictive demands of the society in which they live.

It is worth comparing this last point with items 6 and 15 on Maslow's list (pp. 25-6 above).

Perhaps this argument so far can be summarised by quoting an ex-TB patient's experience as given by Rollo May (1967, p. 95):

> Using illness as re-education is illustrated in a letter a patient with tuberculosis wrote to a friend: 'The disease occurred not simply because I overworked or ran athwart some TB bugs, but because I was trying to be something I wasn't. I was

living as the "great extrovert", running here and there, doing three jobs at once, and leaving undeveloped and unused the side of me which would contemplate, would read and think and "invite my soul" rather than rushing and working at full speed. The disease comes as a demand and an opportunity to rediscover the lost functions of myself. It is as though the disease were nature's way of saying "You must become your whole self. To the extent that you do not, you will be ill; and you will become well only to the extent that you do become yourself." ' We may add that it is an actual clinical fact that some persons, viewing their illnesses as an opportunity for re-education, become more healthy both psychologically and physically, more fulfilled as persons, after a serious illness than before.

For the social worker to collaborate effectively with the client so that illness becomes a re-educative experience, the following need to be borne in mind.

(1) As illness is often a temporary respite from the conditions of existence, the client needs to be encouraged to talk and think about his personal and social situation and the changes in life-style, occupation and surroundings that he spontaneously feels might be more natural to him. Restructuring the self-concept cannot happen unless this process starts and cannot be done for somebody by an external agent.

(2) It is the relationship which is the instrument. The support or 'holding' that Lomas emphasises is incompatible with 'impersonal' role behaviour. The agent, therefore, has to feel free to show care, concern and love for the sick person.

(3) The agent has an interpretative role as indicated by Wolff above. This requires, on the part of the agent, a knowledge of the relationship between situational stress and illness (see Arthur, 1971); also an understanding of the relationship between body and mind as outlined by Reich (see pp. 30-1 above) and as, for example, emphasised by Schutz (1973).

Self-actualisation in marriage

In Jourard's book *The Transparent Self* (1964) there is a chapter on personal growth in marriage which is a worthwhile introduction to this subject and underlines the difficulties in, and opportunities for, helping married people towards personal growth. He says (pp. 37-8):

> Many couples are terrified at growth, change in either themselves or in their spouses. This dread of growth manifests itself in many forms. One of the earliest signs that a person has outgrown a role in which he has been cast by the other person is a sense of boredom, of restlessness, of stultification, or boredom at the sameness of the other. He feels that he would like to be different, but fears that if he expresses his difference, he will either lose love or hurt his spouse. A wife may have been passive, dependent, helpless early in the marriage, and was easily won by a dominant man whose identity as a man was reinforced by her helplessness. In time, she may discover that she has actually become more self-reliant, less eager to please, more able to assert difference. But if she is herself, expresses herself, she may render her spouse very insecure. If she has not consolidated her growth gains, her husband's reaction may frighten her back into the role in which *he* finds her most comfortable.

The real dilemma to which Jourard refers here is well illustrated by the case of Mrs A., who after twenty-five years of marriage, and four children, is now seeking within marriage the autonomy which she feels has been lost over the last twenty-five years. Her husband has a responsible organisational position in charge of many staff and during the period in which she was struggling to find herself as an individual, she had the following dream.

She dreamed that she gave a locket or amulet to a chief who was surrounded by his followers. Then, later, she wanted this object back. She got it back, but was chased by the chief and his followers through a seemingly never-ending series of rooms. In the dream, she experienced tremendous anxiety and fear while being chased in this way and woke up from the dream, screaming.

The difficulties in dream interpretation are well known, but the counsellor is often presented with such material and must do what he can with it. In this case, the dream, within the context of what the client has already disclosed about her current marital situation, is remarkably unambiguous. The reader familiar with existential literature will recognise in the symbol of the locket the characteristic way in which in fantasy or dream 'wholeness' or the 'self' is often represented. He will also recognise the anxiety or fear as the existential anxiety, which as both Goldstein and May have pointed out, is the inescapable accompaniment of all attempts to break out of existing patterns of life and to move forward into new levels of functioning. It is reassuring and confirming if this individual can be helped to see that her unconscious has accurately reflected back to her her present situation. She wants to be herself again (within marriage, it must be emphasised; she has no thoughts about divorce) and asking for the locket back symbolises this. But, equally, the nightmare quality of the chase represents the anxiety she is feeling at the time, knowing full well that her husband feels threatened, and is hostile to the new person she is becoming. This anxiety has to be accepted for it accompanies all significant growth (see p. 36 above).

For many years the Marital Unit of the Tavistock Clinic has recognised how much more readily personal growth in marriage can be facilitated if both partners are in a joint relationship with the worker or counsellor. The Group Experience movement, and, in particular, the Encounter Group movement, has pioneered the growth of Couples' Workshops in which both partners, along with other partners, participate. The possibilities in marriage for personal growth, which Jourard emphasises, have probably not been realised yet to any significant extent.

Trevor Mumby, Director of Interface, has articulated the philosophy of his Family Pairs Workshops as follows:

Couples often erode each other's individuality without recognising the process and consequently adopt a life-style of excessive compromise neither person being able to articulate the *extent* to which they *feel* their 'sacrifice' but carrying on with an inner world of unspoken, but acted out, frustration because of their sense of impeded personal growth.

His strategy is to take the couples through a series of exercises and experiences devised in such a way as to help them; first, to regain their sense of individuality; second, to re-learn how relationships with the opposite sex are made; third, to remake their relationship with their own partner; fourth, to share their experiences with the group as a whole; fifth, to work on 'blocks' in their relationship; and sixth, to help each couple to devise a development plan for their relationship.

Summary

In this chapter, we have considered counselling and group work, in particular, as loci in which personal growth can be facilitated. We have also looked at illness as an occasion for self-discovery and reorientation. Finally, the roles of man and woman in marriage have been considered in relation to self-actualisation. For reasons of space and direct relevance, no mention has been made of various other methods or contexts by which and in which personal growth can be facilitated, for example, by the kind of leadership one gives in educational settings or in organisational life. The reader is referred to *Client-Centred Therapy* (1965) by Rogers and his colleagues for a discussion of the relevance of the methods we have been considering here to these and other fields.

4

An assessment of self-actualisation theories

So far in this book we have considered the work of authors who have emphasised the notion of the self-concept and its role in the development towards self-actualisation. The reader will have noted the variety of terms used by authors, namely, creative becoming (Allport), the fully functioning person (Rogers), individuation (Jung), autonomy (Angyal), world-openness (Schachtel), all of which when examined have a great deal in common with each other and with Maslow's term self-actualisation.

It will not have escaped the reader either that the term 'self' is used in often confusing and contradictory ways. For example, in the term 'self-concept', 'self' seems to be synonymous with 'ego', whereas 'self-actualisation' uses the word 'self' to mean an as yet unrealised self. Much the least confusing is Jung's use of the word 'ego' for the conscious, current personality and the term 'self' for the inner core which has a directing influence over the 'ego', provided that the individual has learned to listen to it and *be* influenced by it (see p. 29 above). Existential writers have coined the term 'authentic self' to draw a sharper distinction between the inner core and the other socially learned and conditioned self.

Kierkegaard, Heidegger, Sartre and others appear to be saying that there is an inner self which is authentic and a false self which is a series of adaptations to social pressures. D. W. Winnicott in his studies of infant development came to think that a split of this kind lies at the centre of the personality as the child struggles to integrate his own urges with his mother's demands. R. D. Laing's view of the self presented in his early books is much like this.

If there is a real self and a false self, our concern in this book must be with the nature of the real self. Can we say that this is a concern of the psychologist, while the sociologist can only speak of the false self, the person as a social construct? Such a division of labour soon creates its own problems, but it may be a useful starting point. It must be transcended by a view that sees the individual as constantly testing, rejecting, assimilating and integrating the various items of his social experience. G. H. Mead was a philosophical sociologist of the early twentieth century whose works are increasingly influential. He distinguishes between 'I' and 'me' and sees 'I' as processing all that has been experienced into an organised form, which then becomes 'me'.

The reader is referred to Ralph Ruddock's very detailed and perceptive treatment of the 'self' and its relation to personality, identity, role and self-realisation in his essay 'Conditions of personal identity' (1972).

The existential critique (Frankl)

Frankl, the founder of logotherapy, whose views on counselling are considered above (pp. 49-53) has taken up a critical position towards 'self-actualisation' (1969, pp. 37-8):

Self-actualisation is not man's ultimate destination. It is not even his primary intention. Self-actualisation, if made an end in itself, contradicts the self-transcendent quality of human existence. Like happiness, self-actualisation is an effect, the effect of meaning fulfilment. Only to the extent to which man fulfils a meaning out there in the world, does he fulfil himself. If he sets out to actualise himself other than fulfil a meaning, self-actualisation immediately loses its justification.

I would say that self-actualisation is the unintentional effect of life's intentionality. No one has ever put this more succinctly than the great philosopher Karl Jaspers when he said: 'What man is, he has become through that cause which he has made his own'.

My contention that man loses any ground for self-actualisation if he cares for it is perfectly in accordance with Maslow's own views, since he admits himself that the 'business of self-actualisation' can best be carried out 'via a commitment to an important job'. In my view, excessive concern with self-actualisation may be traced to a frustration of the will to meaning. As the boomerang comes back to the hunter who has thrown it only if it has missed its target, man, too, returns to himself and is intent upon self-actualisation only if he has missed his mission.

Frankl's comments are borne out by the uneasy feeling one sometimes gets when sitting in a group of people discussing, for example, Maslow's or Rogers's theories. One hears individuals talking of themselves in a way which implies that they regard themselves as self-actualising. One has the feeling that the last person who would ever claim to be self-actualising is the clearly self-actualising person. I think Frankl's criticisms must stand, with some modification; over-preoccupation with self-actualisation may be a substitute for really working towards a goal or may represent an absence of personal fulfilment. Indeed, Maslow himself records the embarrassment of certain potential subjects he approached, and was obliged to gather most of his data indirectly through spouses, relations and close acquaintances.

Nevertheless, if human science is to be complete, we must be allowed to investigate and theorise about the higher forms of human motivation, provided that we do not become so preoccupied with the concept that we never get around to doing anything about it personally. The strictures that Frankl applies to 'self-actualisation' are also applied by some to the preoccupation now-adays with group experience, personal growth and artificially induced self-transcendent experiences. As the author said in another context, 'it will take us some time to accept ... that there is nothing blasphemous in defining self-actualising behaviour and in seeking ways to compensate for the fact that spontaneous growth towards self-actualisation only happens to a fortunate few' (Shaw, 1972, p. 150). What are really under attack from some quarters are both the attempt to understand optimal functioning and also the attempt to make our approach to its achievement more systematic and practical.

Coan's critique of the theories of optimal personality

One very systematic attempt to evaluate the various criteria of the optimal personality is by Richard Coan (1974). Coan gave a battery of tests covering, amongst others, the cognitive, emotional and other behavioural traits that appear in various definitions of optimal functioning to a sample of several hundred college students.

Multivariate analysis was then applied to the subsequent series to elucidate the first- and second-order factors. This research design was carried out with the care and precision one would expect of a former student, and later associate, of R. B. Cattell.

Coan points out that his method of investigation is a necessary corrective to the methods typified, on the one hand, by Maslow, and, on the other, by Rogers. Maslow's close investigation of a small sample, rigorously selected, revealed a combination of traits (see pp. 24-6 above) that *may* turn out to be a function of the peculiarities of that particular sample. Rogers's method based, in the first instance, on observing the course of therapy and its outcome must contain the *possibility* that the therapeutic procedure has a shaping effect on the constellation of traits that emerges. Coan's method, however, is an objective attempt to discover the main dimensions (factors) present in a tremendous variety of measured cognitive, emotional and behavioural elements and to see whether these factors are correlated together in some individuals in a way that matches the descriptions by Maslow, Rogers and others of 'self-actualising' people and whether their descriptions leave out or overlook other aspects of the same people.

His analysis and conclusions are of importance to the humanistic psychology movement. He found seven second-order factors, i.e. statistically distinct dimensions of personality. Each of these has been given a label that describes very briefly the common characteristic of the variety of measured traits that make up the factor. These are:

(1) Restrictive *v.* fluid orientation.
(2) General discomfort.
(3) Uncritical openness (enthusiastic attitude to novelty).
(4) Refined openness (willingness to face new and complex experiences).
(5) Stability.
(6) General intelligence.
(7) Expressiveness.

There are important correlations between some of these factors; for example, Factors 2 and 4 are positively correlated, indicating that a certain amount of distress tends to accompany a willingness to face new and complex experiences. Conversely Factors 3 and 5 are negatively correlated, indicating that the uncritical acceptance of novelty makes for a lack of stability in the personality. To the first of these two examples Coan attaches particular importance, viz. that the sort of openness which, for example, Rogers advocates (see p. 26 above) seems to carry with it, as a sort of liability, experiences of distress and the experience of feelings of loss of control over one's feelings, sensations and thoughts.

He draws a number of conclusions from his research. Of these, the most important for our discussion are the following:
(a) That self-insight, openness to experience and proneness to subjective distress are related.
(b) That openness and subjective distress are related negatively to various forms of experienced control.
(c) That there is no evidence of a unitary dimension that might be viewed as a general factor of personality integration or self-actualisation.

He adds that because of his finding that some desirable characteristics (e.g. openness and freedom from discomfort) are apparently mutually incompatible, we might do better to stop thinking in terms of one optimal personality pattern and think of a variety of patterns that are suited to a variety of purposes.

The two main patterns that he sees in his data are:
(a) Openness, fluidity, permeability and accessibility.
(b) Deliberate control, restriction of attention, and systematic thought and action.

He adds that, in his sample, those who best represent the first attitude are *not*, at the same time, usually the people who best exemplify the second attitude. Coan concludes that a balanced combination of the two attitudes is an obvious desideratum but that, in his sample, at least a few subjects seem to have achieved this balance. In short, a productive life seems possible with either extensive self-awareness or very meagre self-awareness, though, as he readily says, the ability to switch flexibly from the first attitude (e.g. openness to ideas) to the second (e.g. to follow them through systematically) is the most productive of all.

Perhaps openness and control are to be thought of as phases of involvement. We have to be open and uncertain to some extent about every new thing, and we have to move towards closure. If a bus arrives with an unexpected number, we are anxious, but must rapidly close the situation with a decision to board or not. That takes seconds—other situations, for instance, vocational or marital ones, may take years in moving towards closure. The anxiety and discomfort will be correspondingly prolonged. This should remind us that such traits as anxiety or hostility, which appear to be expressions of the self-system, are often to be understood as outcomes of the interpersonal system.

The reader will recall that we discussed above (p. 33) the work of Andreas Angyal which made the particular point that *differentiation* followed by *integration* is a characteristic feature of all developmental progress, whether in the child or in the mature adult. In view of Coan's conclusions, Angyal's words are worth repeating:

> The evolution of any whole takes place in successive stages of differentiation and the re-imbedding of the differentiated parts with the whole. Differentiation always includes a kind of disequilibrium because it is a stage that leads beyond the present status of the whole. The process of differentiation is normally followed by a process of assimilation or re-imbedding whereby the whole itself changes to some extent.

It will be noted that this accords also with Coan's observations of the amount of distress and disorientation that seems an indispensable part of an attitude of openness to experience. Thus we can say that though Maslow and Rogers have perhaps not made this specific point (i.e. differentiation followed by integration) strongly enough, others, notably Angyal, have, and Coan's conclusions endorse its importance.

In the present climate engendered by the desire to apply behavioural science to practical situations we can see examples of programmes which emphasise flexibility, i.e. the ability to switch *from* openness to ideas *to* systematic examination and use of these ideas. In the technique known as 'brain storming', task groups are encouraged, first of all, not to evaluate ideas but simply to generate them; this stage is followed by a further one in which the many ideas generated are then examined for their practical relevance to the problem in hand. Perhaps, however, the most systematic attempt to incorporate *both* openness *and* purposeful thinking with a human development programme for adults lies in the work of C. R. Kelley (1971) of the Interscience Research Institute in Connecticut, USA.

The first part of Kelley's programme looks like a 'traditional' encounter group, in which individuals are helped to make contact with their own feelings that they have become alienated from and to experience them. He is however very aware of the risks that are involved, in particular the subjective distress on which Coan laid so much emphasis. He says (ibid., p. 60):

> To come alive in feeling can make one's work, marriage and way of life each more significant, full and deep and much more rewarding. It can also make any or all three of these unendurable. When one learns to open his eyes emotionally, he may not like what he sees. To come alive in an emotionally deadened world can be painful and disorienting. Mechanical work and superficial human relationships are no longer adequate. A student may no longer fit into the life pattern he has established and yet not be ready to establish another. The problem is felt most poignantly at the dawning of the realisation, before one is sure of the true nature and extent of the problem, and so cannot reasonably take action on it.

Unlike others in this field, Kelley does not simply aim for the limited objective of putting an individual in touch with his feelings. He believes that the individual needs help to put any new self-knowledge to work in his own life. He says (p. 61):

> To realise one's potential, to establish and achieve one's rational objectives, feelings must not only be developed, experienced and expressed, they must be organised and given direction. The energy of even an expanded consciousness must find its proper creative channel, or else be dissipated and signify nothing. Learning feeling is of immense importance, but is in itself not enough for man to live by. Animals live by feeling and instinct; purpose is required for a truly human level of existence.

The second part of Kelley's programme is, therefore, an 'education in purpose' just as the first part is an 'education in feeling'. He calls it a 'confrontation' group; in it the individual 'student', having worked out his personal objectives at an earlier 'workshop' weekend, meets with other 'students' for the purpose of monitoring his own progress and being involved in monitoring the progress of others. The exercise, as Kelley describes it, takes on some of the characteristics of a 'Synanon' group (the former drug addicts' self-help groups). But, in fact, Kelley is here recognising the age-old principle that people need the support of a group when involved in considerable behaviour change; this is a principle recognised by religious leaders and change-agents in many different settings.

Kelley rightly points out that 'education in feeling' and 'education in purpose' are in many respects opposed; spontaneity opposes self-control; tenderness militates against toughness; emotional freedom restricts intellectual clarity; and so on. Yet for human potential to be realised, a reconciliation of these opposites has to take place (p. 67):

> Feeling without purpose is life without direction or goal, and as such is less than fully human. The purposeless individual is fundamentally impotent, without control over his environment, for control is an expression of purpose.... [But] Volitional activity, insufficiently balanced with feeling, becomes mechanical and joyless as its possessor chronically curbs the free movement of his body's creative energy; in time the capacity for spontaneous emotion may be virtually destroyed.

Enough has now probably been said to underline the fact that in some parts of the human potential movement at least there is a recognition of the importance of combining openness with purposiveness in human development. If further evidence is needed the reader is reminded of our discussion in chapter 2 of Allport's emphasis on the importance of 'propriate striving' in 'creative becoming'. It might be mentioned that Coan's subjects were college students, a group that Maslow felt were unpromising for research into self-actualisation. This is probably of some significance. One could hazard a guess that in earlier stages of life, one tends to follow one's natural bent—that is, one's preference may be *either* for openness *or* for deliberate control and restriction of attention. It is probably only later in the life-cycle, if at all, that one deliberately comes to foster the less natural of the two attitudes. Hence Coan's conclusion that his subjects tended to favour one at the expense of the other.

A further word is required regarding Coan's finding that openness to experience tends to be correlated with experiences of internal distress and with experiences of loss of control over thoughts and feelings. This evidence should not be disregarded. It is probably true, for example, that creative artists (e.g. Van Gogh) who have opened up themselves to all kinds of experiences have been broken by them. Also we know that the lowering of protective barriers as in 'acid trips' has resulted in an inrush of disturbing experiences which individuals are sometimes not able to cope with. The 'open' individual is vulnerable in a way that the 'armoured' person is not. Much of the evidence points to the importance of supportive individuals especially in situations where people are opening themselves up for the first time. Rogers's remarks on this in the context of encounter groups (1971, p. 155) are reassuring in this regard. And speaking of the fully functioning person he says, 'He is more open to his feelings of fear and discouragement and pain. He is also more open to his feelings of courage and tenderness and of awe' (1967, p. 188).

Second thoughts on Maslow's hierarchy of needs

In chapter 2 we considered Maslow's hierarchy. He traced out a pattern of need-development (p. 24) through physiological needs, safety needs, belongingness and love needs, and needs for esteem, respect and status. If these needs are regularly gratified, then a pattern of meta-motivation comes into play, i.e. the need to actualise one's unique potentialities comes into the foreground increasingly. However, in an article in 1967 (reprinted 1973), Maslow said, 'Meta-motivation now seems not to ensue automatically after basic-need gratification' (p. 94).

In an interview given shortly before his death, Maslow was asked what the implications of this fact were for his theory of self-actualisation. He replied (Frick, 1971, p. 37):

> You get people who are in the beautiful need-gratifying situation and yet get a kind of value-pathology. That is, it's possible to be loved and respected, etc., and even so, to feel cynical and nihilistic, and to feel there's nothing worth working for.... Especially in younger rather than older people, you can see this. It's sort of a loss of nerve, and I think we're at this point where the traditional culture has broken down altogether.

Maslow goes on to underline the fact that this is so for some individuals but not all and that value-disturbances, e.g. cynicism, nihilism, hopelessness and pessimism, are at the root of this, and he is thinking particularly of the 'drop-out' from society.

Maslow clearly felt that important corrections to his theory were needed but was unable, so far as we know, to resolve this dilemma before his death in 1970. He says in the same interview (p. 39):

> That's one of the things I'm working on. I'm now in this stage of trying to work out the vocabulary and to crystallise it in my own thoughts. Broadly, it's pro-life and pro-death. There are many other overlapping terms; the winner and the loser, the striver and the non-striver, the success and the failure type, the weak struggler or the active and passive.

Maslow admits that the motivation factors beyond the stages of basic need gratification are clearly more complex than he had envisaged when he formulated his original theory. One new category he devised was the 'merely healthy', as distinct from the 'transcenders'. These people are basically gratified, neurosis-free and using some of their capacities well, but by contrast with other self-actualisers, seem not to have peak-experiences, and are very identified with the values of their own culture.

In an article entitled 'Theory Z' (1973), Maslow developed very fully his catalogue of the differences between the 'merely healthy' and the 'transcenders'. The 'merely healthy' do a very good job of what has to be done in the world; are strong personalities; have clear personal objectives; function well in pursuit of these objectives; and they understand their own strengths and weaknesses well. The 'transcenders', however, seem to have developed beyond these traits, good though they are. They are convinced that 'peak-experiences' are the most important events in their lives; they are innovators; are often less happy than the 'merely healthy' ones; the acquisition of knowledge fosters in them a sense of 'mystery'; they understand better the poetic and figurative use of language and can be remarkably objective about themselves. Also they are 'post-ambivalent', i.e. experience strong love unmixed with the usual element of hate; and they have resolved to their own satisfaction many of the dichotomies that plague ordinary people, e.g. rationality-impulse, masculine-feminine, duty-pleasure, science-religion and co-operation-competition.

The implication of this distinction between the 'merely healthy' and the 'transcenders' is that the hierarchy of needs may now be considered as having six levels:

'transcenders' ⎫ self-actualisation
'merely healthy' ⎬ needs

esteem and respect needs
belongingness and love needs
safety needs
physiological needs

The 'merely healthy', one can say, are characterised by congruence between self and experience. However, as Rogers indicates, the self-concept of any self-actualising person is always fluid, never static; hence the possibility that the state of 'mere health' may give rise to further progress and the achievement of the type of meta-motivation which Maslow calls 'transcendent'.

Maslow's later thoughts also emphasised far more than his earlier ones the importance of the cultural environment in facilitating, or holding back, self-actualisation. He says (1973, p. 342):

> the meta-needs seem to me to be instinctoid, that is, to have
> an appreciable hereditary, species-wide determination. But
> they are potentialities rather than actualities. Culture is
> definitely and absolutely needed for their actualisation;
> but also culture can fail to actualise them, and indeed this
> is just what most known cultures actually seem to do and to
> have done throughout history.

One must add that we would expect considerations like class differences, role-deformation, organisational demands on individuals, and types of professional 'personas' to either hinder or facilitate the growth of individuals towards functioning in a 'self-actualising' way.

A sociological point of view

Perhaps we should recognise, before taking our explanation of the concept of self any further, that the sociologists have put forward some very fundamental propositions about the individual, and even about the self. 'Alienation' is a widely used term. It has a long history and tremendous breadth of application. All religious doctrines have claimed that most men and women are alienated from their own inner essence and that the breach can only be healed by openness to grace from a cosmic source. Marx saw the individual as the product of a historical process by which he became alienated from his work, from the product of his work, from his fellow workers and from the natural order. Most great artists have seen man as alienated from his creativity, capacity for play and aesthetic response. Others have said we are alienated from our bodies. There is enough truth in all of these assertions to command some assent from most people. The implications are disturbing. It may be that what we take as the self is no more than a desiccated fragment of what might have been, and may yet be.

In more immediate terms, sociologists have studied the consequences for the individual of occupying various roles, especially work roles. They point out that a man is usually defined by what he does, and that he then takes this as what he is. 'I am a soldier', 'I am a priest', 'I am a social worker'—all of these are roles which easily become identities. People may resist this process but find it forced upon them. 'I applied for supervisory training but they wouldn't have me, a fitter is what I am and what I'll be all my life, I suppose.' T. T. ten Have (1973) points out that professional roles develop or enrich the personality but by middle life the manual worker's personality is subject to progressive impoverishment. The implications for any view of life based on a concept of self-realisation are great. It serves to remind us that we have to work out our temporal destiny within the social order, and that our circumstances may develop, deform or destroy us.

For social workers the argument may be stated thus. Granted that most clients need money and shelter first, they also need roles which accord to them some recognition as a base for identity. These will be work roles and family roles for most people. Many problems that reach the social services originate from a lack of a role. Unemployed young and middle-aged people, the retired, the handicapped and those of least ability and education are most at risk. In what form is the self to be realised by such people? There are answers to this question, but we need to make them more explicit.

In her survey of the literature on optimal human functioning (1958), Marie Jahoda found six major characteristics which could be regarded as constituting the essential definition of optimal functioning. One of these she labels 'a degree of independence of social influences'. This would mean the ability to make autonomous decisions rather than simply to react to present stimuli and the general ability to be independent of the social milieu in which a person lived.

Sociological literature, however, as has been pointed out above, emphasises the extent to which an individual is a product of the culture he lives in and is defined by that culture. Berger and Luck-

mann (1971) have put this view into a dialectical process. They set out the following three propositions:
(1) Society is a human product
(2) Society is an objective reality
(3) Man is a social product.

Thus, although society has been, in the first instance, created by man, it becomes an objective reality in its own right and, as such, exerts an influence on its creators and their descendants, moulding them into certain unmistakeable patterns. As Berger and Luckmann say, 'the product acts back upon the producer'. If this dialectical process is taken seriously, then to what extent can we expect an individual to be able to realise his 'authentic self' as has been argued throughout this book. Berger and Luckmann go on to argue (pp. 77-8) that:

> the institutions are *there*, external to him, persistent in their
> reality, whether he likes it or not. He cannot wish them away.
> They resist his attempts to change or erode them. They
> have coercive power over him, both in themselves, by the
> sheer force of their facticity, and through the control
> mechanisms that are attached to the most important of
> them. The objective reality of institutions is not diminished
> if the individual does not understand their purpose or their
> mode of operation. He may experience large sectors of the
> social world as incomprehensible, perhaps oppressive in their
> opaqueness, but real nonetheless.

Thus the individual has demands made upon him and it is in the context of these demands that he either finds his needs satisfied or frustrated.

As human organisations (*Gesellschaften*) are in some important respects like societies (*Gemeinschaften*) in miniature, and as most of us spend our active adult lives in the context of them, perhaps we can see the force of the sociological argument by using organisational experience as an example. The parallel is not exact but it may be instructive. Argyris (1965) says that organisations have traditionally been run by 'directive' leadership, thus fostering dependence and passivity among the workers at various levels. As mature adults favour autonomy and activity (see chapter 2 above), an environment of this kind creates, in many, feelings of conflict, frustration and failure.

Individuals defend themselves against these experiences in a number of negative and positive ways (from the organisation's point of view). Chief among the negative ways would be: leaving the organisation; lapsing into apathy and alienation; or repressing many needs and seeking only the satisfaction of economic and material needs through work.

A more positive adaptation from the organisation's point of view would be climbing the organisation ladder where the pressure towards dependency is less, or even becoming an 'organisation man'; this is the man who, according to Whyte (1956), over-identifies with the goals of the organisation and while sacrificing some of his own uniqueness obtains the satisfactions of success, status and the sense of belonging to a purposeful whole.

Argyris argues that if self-actualisation is to be possible for larger numbers of people then a new kind of organisation is necessary which lays more emphasis on the needs of mature people as well as the necessary demands of the organisation upon the individual. He asserts that more authentic relationships are necessary between superiors and subordinates and between peers, as well as strategies of job-enlargement and job-enrichment. In these ways workers will come to experience more of the satisfactions necessary to mature life, i.e. autonomy, activity, self-development, a long-term perspective, and the opportunity to exercise and develop a variety of skills and abilities.

If we return to the dialectical model we referred to earlier, we can see in dialectical terms the effect of a policy that Argyris as an organisational theorist is advocating. Also this process is a logical possibility at the cultural level, even though the pervasiveness and power of a culture is of a quite different order (see figure 8).

All dialectical theorists should recognise that there is, logically, no end to a dialectical process, so that the triad that Berger and Luckmann specify is abstracted from a larger process, mostly as yet unrealised. Man, by his capacity to reflect upon his experience, can, unless we take a determinist view, set in motion the next stage of the dialectical process. This is continually happening on the organisational level, and is a logical possibility on the cultural level.

We must accept that individual self-actualisation can be seriously hampered, and in some instances completely negated, by the demands made upon individuals by the organisations or societies in which they exist. As Maslow said (see p. 75 above), most cultures hold back self-actualisation. It is for this reason that many of those interested in the development of human potential have become

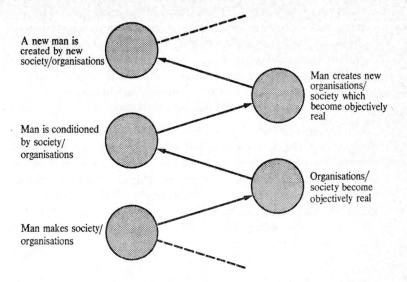

A new man is created by new society/organisations

Man creates new organisations/ society which become objectively real

Man is conditioned by society/ organisations

Organisations/ society become objectively real

Man makes society/ organisations

FIGURE 8   *The dialectical process in organisation and culture*

convinced of the need for separate communities or private Utopias in which both individual needs and social demands are recognised and self-actualisation becomes a real possibility for the group's members. Equally, as original socialisation took place in primary groups (e.g. family and peer groups), then the 'new man' can only emerge through new primary group experiences. Argyris has argued (1965) that organisational development necessitates the setting up of consultation groups, which are primary groups of colleagues with a programme of mutual self-development. The many experiential groups, which are such a feature of the personal growth movement, are an expression of the same principle.

One of the fundamental weaknesses of the case for human development towards self-actualisation is that it often stresses only one side of the equation. Unless man is actively concerned with the restructuring of his organisational and social environment while restructuring himself, he is, unless in extremely favourable circumstances, unlikely to get very far.

G. H. Mead has expressed this point of view most fully when he says (quoted by Ruddock, 1972, pp. 109-10):

Human society, we have insisted, does not merely stamp
the pattern of its organised social behaviour upon any one

79

of its social members ... it also gives him a mind ... and this mind enables him in turn to stamp the pattern of his further developing self (further developing through his mental activity) upon the structure or organisation of human society, and thus in a degree, to reconstruct and modify in terms of his self the general pattern of social or group behaviour in terms of which his self was originally constructed.

Equally, a sociological perspective which concentrates on a segment of a dialectical process and which ignores the as yet unrealised parts of this process is bound to emphasise the existing social reality and its oppressive power. This can foster a sense of hopelessness and helplessness on two levels; on the one hand, we may come to feel that culture is not open to change in a dynamic way; and on the other the individual may come to feel himself a prisoner of existing objective social reality.

Empirical studies of self-theory

It was stated in chapter 2 that a self-concept which is congruent with experience is the key to continuing self-actualisation. As was said, the self-concept includes one's views about one's characteristics and abilities; also views about the nature of one's relations to other people and one's environment; views about the values one gives to various experiences and objects; and the positive or negative values one places on various ideals or purposes. When one's behaviour, feelings, thoughts and relationships are in line with these self-views, one can admit them to awareness without distortion. When they are not, one usually engages in strategies of self-justification or denial or distortion, in an attempt to dismiss them as uncharacteristic aberrations (e.g. 'I don't know what came over me!') or as the results of coercion by others (e.g. 'Now see what you've made me do!').

Rogers argues, therefore, that the effect of a counselling relationship which does something positive for a client, is to reduce the gap between his self-concept and his experience, thereby restructuring the self-concept in a more realistic form. The question we need to ask, therefore, is whether there is any empirical evidence that this actually happens within an individual who is, say, in a counselling relationship with a counsellor. Moreover, if measurable behaviour changes take place in such a relationship, is there evidence that these changes are due to changes in the structure of the self, as asserted in the theory?

In an interesting study carried out at the Counselling Center of the University of Chicago (Rogers and Dymond, 1954) 29 clients, dealt with by 16 different therapists, were carefully monitored throughout a period which lasted from two months before therapy began to twelve months after the therapy had been completed. A control group of individuals not in therapy and roughly equivalent in age and socio-economic status were monitored over an equivalent period.

The method for measuring changes in the self-concept was the Q-sort technique. Each subject was given a hundred cards on each of which were statements like 'I am a submissive person', 'I don't trust my emotions', 'I feel relaxed and nothing bothers me', 'I am afraid of sex', 'I have an attractive personality'. The subject was asked to sort these cards into nine piles, ranging from those items most characteristic of himself or herself to those least characteristic. At the same time, he was asked to sort them again for the self he would like to be, his ideal self. This procedure was carried out a maximum of four times for each client, i.e. sixty days before therapy, immediately prior to therapy, immediately after therapy, and, finally, after a period of six to twelve months from the completion of therapy.

Rogers (1967, p. 231) draws the following conclusions from this research:

> [it is clear] that profound changes occur in the perceived self of the client during and after therapy; that there is constructive change in the client's personality characteristics and personality structure, changes which bring him closer to the personality characteristics of the well-functioning person; that there is change in directions defined as personal integration and adjustment; that there are changes in the maturity of the client's behaviour as observed by friends. In each instance the change is significantly greater than that found in the control group.... Only in regard to the hypotheses having to do with acceptant and democratic attitudes in relation to others are the findings somewhat confused and ambiguous.

In one specific client in this study, a woman of forty, the correlation between perceived self immediately before and after therapy was 0·39, whereas the correlation between perceived self immediately after therapy and twelve months later was 0·65. (A lower correlation, of course, indicates greater change and higher correlation indicates less change.) Rogers is able to show that this is generally true of all the clients studied in therapy, namely, that the change in the perceived self during therapy is greater than the change in perceived self during the preparation or follow-up periods and significantly greater than the changes in perceived self observed in the control group.

The reader is referred to Rogers (1967, pp. 226-41) and to Rogers and Dymond (1954) for a full account of this research. One weakness of the research, however, is that correlations do not imply cause-effect relationships. Thus, although, the process of therapy is marked by 'constructive change' and this change is reflected in changes in the self-concept, it does not follow that the changes in the self-concept 'caused' the constructive changes. All we are able to say is that the two processes seem to be parallel to each other and that changes in the one will probably be accompanied by changes in the other.

Another relevant piece of research by Raskin (1952) relates to one of Rogers's defining characteristics of the 'fully functioning person'. He has stated that such people find their own values within themselves rather than relying on a value-system derived from their social and cultural environment. The method of 'client-centred therapy' attempts to foster a development towards this method of moral decision by the counsellor refusing to think *for* the client, by his refusal to take responsibility for solving the client's problems, but instead concentrating on thinking through the problems with him.

Raskin devised an equal-appearing-intervals scale ranging from unqualified reliance on the evaluations made by others, at one end, to clear reliance on one's own experience and judgment, as the basic source of values, at the other end. Having tested the scale for reliability, he applied it to a sample of 59 interviews of actual clients which had been taped and which were drawn from all stages of the counselling process, i.e. first interviews, final interviews and in-between interviews. He found that the average scores of clients on this scale for the first interviews was 1·97 and for the final interviews 2·73. (Lower scores indicate an external orientation, higher scores indicate a greater reliance on one's own judgment.) This is a statistically significant difference and indicates that the effect of therapy was to shift a client's locus of evaluation from external to internal sources. Furthermore, in the most successful of these cases, as rated by other objective research carried out on these clients, the shift was from 2·12 in the first interviews to an average of 3·34 in the final interviews, indicating an even sharper shift in the direction hypothesised.

We may conclude that there is empirical evidence, only a little of which has been mentioned here, that the claims of self-theory have an objective basis. Of course, some psychologists have expressed doubts about 'self-report' as a basis for objective measurement. In the research by Rogers and Dymond (1954) mentioned above, use was made of corroborating descriptions of clients by experienced diagnosticians. This part of the study shows the client moving nearer to a picture of himself which is significantly correlated with the view of him taken by an outside observer, while at the beginning of therapy there was a complete absence of correlation between his own self-report and that of the experienced diagnostician.

Summary

We have considered criticisms of self-actualisation and self-theory from psychological and sociological points of view and also looked at empirical evidence both for and against. We concluded that the concept and the theory stand up to these criticisms.

Finally, one ought to comment on the remarkable fact that from a number of independent thinkers in different branches of human science has come a convergence towards the notion of self-actualisation. Cofer and Appley (1964) listed ten major theorists who placed the notion (under some synonym or other) in a central position. The argument from convergence does not, logically, prove that there really is such a drive, but the agreement is impressive and not to be lightly dismissed.

When, for example, Jung was confronted with the evidence from the unconscious that led him to his concept of 'individuation' (the human drive towards unique wholeness: see chapter 2 above), he needed reassurance that his thinking was soundly based. He considered that such an important phenomenon would, even in the pre-psychological era, have become apparent to man in either literary or theological or artistic or scientific form. As he says in his autobiography (Jaffé, ed., 1963, p. 226):

First I had to find evidence for the historical prefiguration of my inner experiences. That is to say, I had to ask myself, 'Where have my particular premises already occurred in history?' If I had not succeeded in finding such evidence, I would never have been able to substantiate my ideas. Therefore, my encounter with alchemy was decisive for me, as it provided me with the historical basis which I had hitherto lacked.

The point of our study is that we do obtain reassurance from finding that there is a consensus of opinion especially among thinkers of the calibre of Allport, Maslow, Goldstein and others. Although this reassurance is no substitute for direct experience and systematic research, it does mean that there is a concept 'self-actualisation' and a body of theory, which we call self-theory, which demands serious consideration.

5
Implications of self-theory for social work

Many social workers are going through a period of soul-searching. They look back to the beginnings of social work in philanthropy and the charitable trusts of the nineteenth century. They recognise them as a point of origin but as implying attitudes that are totally inappropriate today. They also look at the way in which social work was, and still is, deeply influenced by psychoanalysis and ask searching questions about the real value for social work of this influence. They are examining the political implications of social welfare provision and wonder to what extent society has ever really wanted to face the issues of poverty, unemployment, mental disorder, and the role in all this of 'free market' economics. Again, the issue of casework versus community development illustrates a crisis of identity. Also, there are the problems of 'values' in social work. Is it true, for example, that social work has often been the imposition of middle-class values on working-class clients, for whom these values are in many ways irrelevant? And, to mention just one more question at issue, there is the unsolved issue of the relative importance of material help and emotional or psychological help. Is social work about getting wheel-chairs for disabled people or about helping a client to work through antagonistic attitudes to authority? Indeed, should the word 'client', with all that it implies, continue to be used at all?

This is an opportune time, therefore, to consider the contribution that humanistic psychology, self-theory, and, in particular, self-actualisation has to make to this debate. The purpose of this chapter will be to take a number of issues currently the subject of discussion in social work circles and to look at them from the standpoint taken in this book.

Intermediate treatment

In an article in *Social Service News* (1972, p. 14), Chris Andrews says:

> To attempt to define its nature would be, in a way, self-defeating. The definition [of intermediate treatment] would either be so vague as to be meaningless or would restrict its application in such a way that its full potential would be limited.

Later he adds:

> To say Intermediate Treatment is normally carried out in groups, or is activity-based, or community-based, or social work based, or has any other particular characteristic, would exclude a wide field which, for certain children in trouble, may most appropriately meet their needs. It is by remaining undefined that the concept of Intermediate Treatment can remain flexible and sensitive to the needs of every child and able to adjust to changing circumstances and to new thinking.

Another article by Robert Alen (1972) emphasises the fact that the personal relationship between worker and child is the vital element and adds (pp. 9-10):

> Unless children are able to make a personal relationship with a caring person then intermediate treatment will be either a grandiose piece of legislation or an ineffective service. It is vital that children are able to form a personal relationship with a person skilled in child care. One of the fundamentals for intermediate treatment is the failure of children and parents to relate adequately at one level or another.

He sees the attitude of the worker as vital and defines this role as that of a catalyst or facilitator rather than a director or leader.

If we concentrate, as these writers suggest, on the relationship between the worker and the child and if, also, we make the assumption that intermediate treatment will often take place in activity groups of various kinds, then there is a fair amount that can be said about the role of the worker. Social psychological research into behaviour change in groups (see p. 54 above) has led to a considerable body of knowledge about the kind of leadership that produces change. The role of the worker in this kind of group is different from the role of the worker in a personal growth group of the unstructured kind that Rogers favours (see pp. 55-7 above). We are talking here of a worker who has clearer behavioural and attitudinal objectives. His objectives are to foster the ability of the child to make co-operative relationships with the worker and with his peers in the group and to help him to transfer this experience to his own family setting.

Argyris (1969) has spelled out some of the conditions for this sort of change through group experience. In a modified form, suitable for our discussion, these are as follows:

(1) If an individual comes to feel that he is a member of a new 'culture' (i.e. sharing the norms of a new group), then he can be influenced at the three levels of knowledge, feelings and behaviour. In this way one hopes to avoid setting up tensions between new knowledge and existing feelings, which is often the result of a cognitive approach to behavioural change.

(2) The change in the individual from *hostility* to *friendliness* towards the new culture (i.e. consideration of, and co-operation with, others) as a whole must be given priority over emphasis on single items of the re-educative programme.

(3) If an individual does not feel that he is a voluntary member of a group, he will feel more loyalty to his old group and hostility to the new values. Only a new set of values freely chosen will be accepted. Hence, the greatest possible amount of individual choice about which group he will join is necessary.

(4) The atmosphere of the group must be supportive not threatening. The worker naturally helps to create this atmosphere but tries to bring the group to feel that they are all responsible for this.

(5) At the beginning of the group's life the worker encourages members to ventilate their attitudes towards working together. He believes that thoughts, feelings and behaviour needing change must be brought to the surface, for if they remain buried, they stay blurred.

(6) Once these thoughts and feelings have been expressed, reactions and opposite views must be forthcoming, preferably from other group members, but, if necessary, from the worker himself. The worker's main assumption here is that the most effective influence upon an individual is from other group members, but he has a responsibility to wield influence if reinforcement of existing attitudes rather than change is taking place.

(7) The worker will sometimes find himself in a teaching role, giving

the group the information it needs in order to make its decisions and pursue its task objectives. However, it is most effective when the information is supplied at the time when it is needed by the group and hence is perceived by the group as vital and important.
(8) The worker tries to foster a sense of belonging in the group and to create a group which is attractive to its members. Both of these factors make a group much more potent in its influence over members.
(9) The worker encourages the group to perceive its own needs, thus generating pressure from within the group itself towards change and development.
(10) When learning about the benefits of co-operation and consideration have taken place, the worker takes time both with individuals and the group as a whole to discuss its application beyond the group to their family and school situations.

In the primary groups which are common to all of us (e.g. the family, peer groups and working groups), we develop our original self-concept. If learning of the type envisaged in intermediate treatment is to be effective, it must lead to a restructuring of the self-concept (e.g. different values, and new attitudes to self and others). By creating a new primary group of the type we have discussed, we are making possible a process of unlearning and re-learning, in a situation which is in some measure comparable to those (i.e. the original primary groups) in which the original and inadequate learning took place.

Values and social work

Leonard (1966, p. 72) in a discussion of cultural values and social work says: 'all agencies even those whose powers appear to be entirely persuasive are concerned with the modification of human behaviour in the direction of certain cultural norms.' He adds (p. 73):

> There is a tendency to assume, unthinkingly, that the social worker's values are in the last resort more *right* or more *natural*. The problems which may arise over a clash of values between the social worker and the client can be illustrated by considering the implications of different class attitudes to child-rearing and parental roles.

He rightly points out that effective social work can only be done if there is a recognition of the possibility of value-conflicts of various kinds between worker and client: 'The fact that a social worker's values are largely middle class in origin does not in itself condemn them, but it does demand care in making decisions which imply the superiority of one value over another' (p. 75).

This kind of dilemma which confronts the social worker is heightened if one takes the view, as the above writer does, that all or most values are the result of cultural conditioning. The emphasis of writers in the self-theory 'school' is different. Both Rogers and Maslow, for example, have remarked on the unmistakeable value-content to be found in human needs and drives when an individual is functioning in an integrated way.

Maslow's views may be set out in the following way. In an article entitled 'The fusion of facts and values' (1973) he felt obliged, as a result of his own observation and research, to question the basic philosophical distinction between fact and value, between *is* and *ought*. Summarising the detailed argument of this paper, he says: the facts themselves carry within their own nature, suggestions about what ought to be done with them' (p. 130). He argues that the more an individual is in possession of the facts, about himself and his own needs, about the demands of his environment, about role-expectations, etc., the more the likelihood that his response to a situation will be appropriate and right for that situation. He quotes with approval Fromm's description of the reverse situation, 'Sickness consists essentially in wanting what is not good for us' (p. 219).

In a further article in the same collection, entitled 'A theory of meta-motivation: the biological rooting of the value life' (1973), he says (p. 336):

> The spiritual or value-life falls well within the realm of nature, rather than being a different and opposed realm. It is susceptible to investigation at once by psychologists and social scientists, and in theory, will eventually become also a problem for neurology, endocrinology, genetics, and biochemistry as these sciences develop suitable methods.

This is a very affirmative statement. The difficulty, of course, is that his conclusion is derived from observation of people who are basic-need-gratified and who are, in his terminology, meta-motivated. By definition, the average social work client is not basic-need-gratified.

Rogers notes a similar phenomenon. He observes that the progress of clients in therapy is marked by a movement towards locating their 'locus of evaluation' within themselves (1967, p. 189):

> In choosing what course of action to take in any situation, many people rely upon guiding principles, upon a code of action laid down by some group or institution, upon the judgment of others ... or upon the way they have behaved in some similar past situation. Yet as I observe the clients whose experiences in living have taught me so much, I find that increasingly such individuals are able to trust their total organismic reaction to a new situation because they discover to an ever-increasing degree that if they are open to their experience, doing what 'feels right' proves to be a competent and trustworthy guide to behaviour which is truly satisfying.

What is the implication of this point of view for social work, and in particular for the value-conflict in social work described above by Leonard? As I noted earlier, neither Rogers nor Maslow is claiming that this intrinsic valuing-process is usually found in people who are subject to gross external deprivation of basic needs, or, indeed, in others who are well-gratified at the basic levels, but who are suffering from the 'meta-pathologies' of despair, nihilism, etc. Rogers, for example, sees the ability developing as individuals restructure their self-concept so that more of their experience can be symbolised in consciousness without distortion. It is probably also true that cultural relativism in values is, and is likely to remain, a firm feature of our class-divided society.

It is clear that an agent who is impressed by the case put forward by Rogers, Maslow and others will wish to be a facilitator. He will want to create the conditions in which the individual client can find his own moral solution. Such an approach would be akin to the counselling method described in chapter 3 above. He will see this as his most favoured approach, because the choice rests where it should, namely, with the client, and because it accords with his own views about the potentiality of individuals. It is clear also that religious presuppositions could lead to a similar orientation.

However, bearing in mind the statutory role of many social workers which means that ultimately a certain responsibility for the client's welfare devolves on them, an agent knows that in other

situations he must use other methods. When a client is fully identified with his own culture, the working-class culture, for example,
the agent would accept that the client's best possibility for social
acceptance in his own culture is to make a choice within the range
of options open to him within the value-system of that culture. The
agent's role then would be to help the client to list the cultural
options open to him and support him while he makes an
appropriate choice.

Finally, with clients who are extremely dependent on the worker
or who are morally confused, perhaps because of their position
midway between two value-systems, an agent may be obliged to
take a more directive stance. This might mean making a value-
choice for the client and then persuading him to adopt it. It is in
situations like this that agents might rightly be accused of imposing
their values on clients, as Leonard suggests. This can never be done
lightly and makes great demands upon an agent for objectivity and
careful thought.

In short, the issue boils down to one of flexibility of approach
on the part of the worker and Table 2 sets out these differences in
style in very simplified form. Social workers cannot help sometimes,
with some clients, being put in the position of making value-choices
for them. Neither can they help being in a society with different
sets of behavioural norms. However, statements to the effect that
all social work is a process of imposing middle-class norms on
working-class people are probably not true. They would only be
true if all clients were in dependence-dominance relations with their
social workers, as perhaps many adolescent clients and some adult
clients are.

The hierarchy of needs as applied to social work

Perhaps the most crucial question a social worker can ask is 'What
are my client's real needs?' Are they external needs or are they
internal needs? Should a social worker concentrate, for example, on
finding his client work and getting him and his family rehoused?
Or, on the other hand, is social work really about helping a client
to resolve internal conflicts which themselves are the real cause of
external adverse conditions and which, if untreated, will bring on
more external problems when the present ones are solved?

No doubt many social workers would say that social work aims
to satisfy both internal and external needs if a worthwhile job is

TABLE 2 *The social worker and the value-choices of clients*

Social Worker style	Client's personality or attitudes	Social worker's task
Facilitative	Autonomous; is experiencing the ability to make satisfactory value-choices.	To create an emotional climate and an intellectual framework within which the client can arrive at his own decisions.
Exploratory	Fully identified with own cultural values.	To help the client to explore the 'cultural options' open to him and to make a reasoned choice.
Persuasive/ Coercive	Dependent on worker; looks to worker for guidance as to the value-choices he should make.	Takes the responsibility for making value-choices for the client and concentrates on persuading him to accept them.

This outline is extremely schematic, leaving out many other possibilities. The arrows on the left-hand side indicate the fact that in moving from the 'facilitative' style towards the 'persuasive/coercive' style we move from a relationship of equality with the client to one of superordination over the client. The questionableness of this latter relationship is really the core of the criticism put forward by Leonard (see p. 88 above) and Cannan (see Introduction).

to be done for the client. J. H. Wallis (1973), however, sees the external orientation and the internal orientation as marking out a division within the social work profession. He summarises thus (p. 77):

These two factions within the casework professions summarise their differences by claiming, on the one hand, 'Basically we are social workers not psychotherapists' or, on the contrary, 'Basically we are dealing with the human nature of individuals, each of whom has a different temperament, a different life-experience, a different scale of values and aims, both conscious and unconscious. Therefore, whether we like it or not, we are dealing with the psychology of the individual'. This dilemma arises again and again in the experience of individual caseworkers, as it does in conferences and in in-service groups. One often hears social workers (voluntary and professional) say 'We are not psychologists. As social workers we must deal with social conditions'. Sometimes they fiercely resist the individual, personal approach as though it were dangerous, unethical or obscene.

Wallis points out, on the basis of listening to many tape-recorded interviews between trainee social workers and clients, that a worker will often switch the discussion from feelings to facts when he feels stuck, or becomes self-conscious or embarrassed during the process of the interview. Generalising from this phenomenon, he argues that counsellors or caseworkers protest that they are not psychotherapists because they find discussion of feelings and inner conflicts disturbing and worrying, while, on the other hand, discussion of factual information and the external or environmental conditions of the client is safer ground.

Furthermore, clients themselves often begin an interview by presenting an external or situational problem as a means of testing out the attitudes of the worker and the 'climate' of the relationship, and may subsequently move on to more intimate topics if they have been reassured by the response the first topic evokes. Wallis argues that here the client is protecting himself in much the same way as the worker is when he emphasises external conditions or switches during an interview to facts from feelings. Internally-oriented caseworkers are prone to regard the 'presenting problem' as unimportant. Wallis retorts that this attitude would often be wrong. Many such problems (e.g. whether to start divorce proceedings or whether to leave a particular job) may be symbols of deeper difficulties but are also urgent and important in their own right.

Whether or not one agrees with Wallis's explanation, and indeed whether or not one agrees with his view that there are 'two factions' in the casework professions, there is a problem over the relative importance of material and emotional needs. Does Maslow's hierarchy of needs offer anything to the discussion about their relative significance?

We noted above (pp. 24-6) Maslow's argument that in states of extreme material deprivation the needs for food, shelter and

93

basic physical survival are paramount. These needs, along with others which we will consider shortly, are labelled by Maslow 'deficiency needs' and he characterises a deficiency need in the following way (1968, p. 22):

(1) its absence breeds illness.
(2) its presence prevents illness.
(3) its restoration cures illness.
(4) under certain (very complex) free choice situations, it is preferred by the deprived person over other satisfactions.
(5) it is found to be inactive, at a low ebb, or functionally absent in the healthy person.

He adds, 'It is these needs which are essentially deficits in the organism, empty holes, so to speak, which must be filled up for health's sake, and furthermore must be filled from without by human beings *other* than the subject' (ibid.).

This case for the salience of 'deficiency needs' supports the case made out by those in social work and other helping professions who argue that collective pressure on the appropriate authorities to rid society of poverty, homelessness and unemployment is the single most important function of all who share a concern for the deprived and who want to see them developing towards full humanity. But equally, the argument that the social worker's role is to be concerned with the feelings, conflicts, relationships and roles of the client, is also supported. For, in Maslow's hierarchy, the needs for security, belongingness and love, and, finally, esteem and self-respect, are also 'deficiency needs'. Their gratification is as necessary as the gratification of material needs. Absence of such gratification equally 'breeds illness', in Maslow's phrase. No motivational distinction, therefore, is made between material and emotional needs, although given that man is a biological organism, it is logical that his physical survival is the precondition for his being able to function psychologically and socially at all. For this obvious reason, the physiological needs are at the base of the motivational pyramid.

There is ample evidence from other sources for the soundness of Maslow's pyramid of deficiency motivation. The physiological and psychological effects of starvation have been studied. Keys *et al.* (1950) studied a group of conscientious objectors during the Second World War who volunteered to serve as subjects for research into the effects of semi-starvation. The researchers noted, over the six months of the programme, that the subjects were unable to continue their intellectual interests owing to their intense preoccupation with food. Their capacity for emotional response was significantly lessened. Humour, singing and whistling disappeared. Conversation at meal times died out and squabbling over petty matters increased. Decreased sociability was a very noticeable effect; or if sociability was maintained, it was limited to a few friends and counterbalanced by extreme hostility towards others. Holmberg (1950), in his field study of the Siriono Indians, whose life is almost entirely spent in hunting for scarce food resources, noted that there is a virtual absence of art, folk tales or mythology in their culture. Concern for truth or beauty does not emerge when a more basic 'deficiency need' is not being gratified.

It is important to note the decline and deterioration in emotional and social activity in the semi-starvation research just mentioned, which supports Maslow's view about the salience of physiological needs when they are not being gratified and the corresponding decline of the higher 'deficiency' needs (i.e. security, belongingness and love, and esteem and self-respect). It is an important part of Maslow's analysis that the 'healthy' (i.e. basic-need-gratified) person has a greater variety of needs than the 'unhealthy' (i.e. basic-need-deprived) person. The conscientious-objector group during the period of the research were characterised by a monotony of interest in food needs. Equally, when an individual has an abundance of food but is deprived, or afraid, of love and personal relationships, then food may come to have an exaggerated positive value for the individual. This fact clearly emerges from Bruch's (1948) study of the psychological aspects of obesity.

However, given a measure of gratification of physiological needs, the 'caring' person must recognise, à la Maslow, that the gratification of the other 'deficiency needs' are as vital to human survival and development. As was stated earlier, no motivational distinction can be made between material and emotional needs, as in the case of the 'two factions' cited by Wallis. The next highest deficiency needs are for safety and security. By this Maslow means the individual's needs for an environment that can be relied on, which reaches a certain level of dependability and order. We are convinced, from the evidence of many child studies, of the importance of the satisfaction of these needs for the infant and the growing child. However, the adolescent and the adult need them too. Rogers has developed a parallel notion of 'psychological safety' as a condition of growth; he says it is a combination of unconditional acceptance, absence of external evaluation, and empathic understanding: 'In this climate you can permit your real self to emerge and to express itself in varied and novel formings as it relates to the world' (1967, p. 358). Social workers who claim to be solely concerned with improving the basic material conditions in which their clients live would also, if pressed, probably agree that they try to provide for their clients the security of a consistent relationship and to this extent, in practice, recognise the importance of security needs.

It is when we consider the 'deficiency needs' for belongingness and love that we encounter what Ralph Ruddock calls 'the need for roles'. He says (1969, p. 27):

> Role requirements are imposed on the child and he has to learn to conform with them. This however is only half the story. The other half concerns the need of the individual, child or adult, to find roles he can play and so secure acceptance from others. Until he finds acceptable roles he can have no sense of relationship to any other person.

Just how serious this need is can be seen in the problems presented to the social worker by the unemployed young person, the deserted wife, the aged person living alone, the unemployed ex-prisoner without family ties and so on. The argument here is that the needs to belong and be loved are usually gratified through the medium of role relationships and the caring person's task is to create conditions in which these needs can usually be met, i.e. by helping the individual to find satisfactory work and family roles. It is true that such a concern on the part of social workers is often construed as merely a socialising or re-socialising role, i.e. to help the individual to conform to what society expects of him. But given the deficiency need for belongingness and love, as it has been defined here, it can be thought of more positively as 'therapy through roles'. This is no argument, of course, for retaining in society roles that deform or roles that restrict personal growth (see Ruddock, ibid., and Jourard, 1964).

The next level of deficiency needs (for prestige, esteem and self-esteem) is involved here. It is usually through the fulfilment of roles, whether in the family or in work, that the individual finds much of the gratification of his needs for the esteem of others and of self-esteem. However, self-esteem as a 'deficiency need' demands considerable attention.

Maslow (1954, p. 91) says:

> Satisfaction of the self-esteem need leads to feelings of self-
> confidence, worth, strength and capability and adequacy,
> of being useful and necessary in the world. But thwarting of
> these needs produces feelings of inferiority, of weakness,
> and of helplessness. These feelings in turn give rise to
> either basic discouragement or else compensatory or
> neurotic trends.

He adds an important proviso (ibid.), considering the fact that much research, following Cooley (1902), emphasised self-appraisal as being largely derived from the appraisal made of one by others:

> We have been learning more and more of the dangers of
> basing self-esteem on the opinions of others rather than on real
> capacity, competence, and adequacy to the task. The most
> stable and therefore most healthy self-esteem is based on
> *deserved* respect from others rather than on external
> fame or celebrity or unwarranted adulation.

It is true that Maslow tends to talk of self-esteem in a global way, as if one were either totally low or high in self-esteem. One individual may have a high level of confidence about his occupational ability, but a lower level of confidence in social relations. Moreover, self-confidence over, say, one's occupational ability may vary from time to time depending on the measure of success one is enjoying at a particular time. This is a commonplace experience. We may, however, fall back on the phrase used by Erikson (see chapter 1 above) and say that every individual needs a favourable ratio of positive over negative self-evaluations if he is to function socially and work competently. When Maslow talks of self-esteem as a 'deficiency need' we may assume that this is what he means. Of all the 'deficiency needs', the need for self-esteem is probably the most difficult for a deprived or disadvantaged client to satisfy. They are often not only people who do not 'believe in' themselves, but also usually people whom society does not 'believe in' either. This last point has been brought home to social workers by the difficulties they have encountered in trying to integrate various groups, e.g. ex-prisoners, the mentally ill, and the handicapped, into the wider community. As Goffman (1968, p. 9) says, they are 'disqualified from full social acceptance'. One of the most successful ways in which disadvantaged individuals have tried to solve this problem is by creating, or having created for them, groups of people with a similar problem, e.g. alcoholics, ex-prisoners, drug addicts, the physically handicapped. In this way the individual can obtain the necessary prestige, acceptance and esteem through the contribution he is able to make to the group's life and activities. For, while we may not totally accept Cooley's view of the 'looking glass self', it is still true that acceptance within a group of peers is a vital need, without which most individuals cannot function.

On the other hand, as Maslow has pointed out (see p. 97 above), self-esteem to be complete needs as a basis an internally derived view of one's real capacities and abilities. Here one encounters in practice the real difficulty presented by the self-hating person, the person who feels chronically unworthy, sometimes expressing this by withdrawal from others, or in other cases by aggressiveness and nastiness towards others. Rogers's quite marked preoccupation with this personality characteristic and his recognition of its key role in stunted development led him to the concept of *unconditional positive regard* (see chapter 2 above) as the crucial attitude of the counsellor or social worker. His assertion of the reality of self-actualising motivation has largely been based on his clinical experience that an atmosphere of acceptance—'caring for the client as a separate person, with permission for him to have his own feelings and experiences, and to find his own meanings in them' (1967, p. 283)—leads individuals to dig down within themselves and to arrive at re-evaluations of themselves. They become able to respect themselves and value themselves. Rogers (1967) has so fully documented this insight that the reader can only be recommended to read it and arrive at a personal judgment about its validity.

Maslow's work on self-esteem is bound up with his concept of the 'syndrome'. He means by a personality syndrome a complex of thought, behaviour, drives and perception that has a common unity and a common purpose. Syndromes have a built-in resistance to change, but when change does take place, it tends to change the syndrome as a whole. In his view, one can think of 'self-esteem' as a syndrome which, in a given individual, may be at a high, middle or low level. He reports an early experiment of his own (1954, p. 41) very similar to some of the behaviour modification schedules we are familiar with today. This resulted in a generalised shift in self-esteem in the lady concerned, affecting the nature of her dreams, the kind of clothes she bought, her attitudes to sex and improved confidence in a variety of social situations.

Enough has probably already been said about the 'need for self-actualisation' which emerges more strongly once the 'deficiency needs' have been regularly gratified. The characteristic of autonomy and independence both of the 'merely healthy' self-actualisers and the 'transcender' self-actualisers is central. It is obvious, therefore, that social work is largely operative at the level of 'deficiency needs' and is concerned with helping those who have not naturally experienced the gratification of the 'deficiency needs' in their family and social life and thus have not naturally moved on to 'growth' motivation. However, the fact of the self-actualising drive broods over all this concern with the 'deficiency needs', for the clear assertion of Rogers, Maslow, Jung, Goldstein and others is that there is a drive to transcend existing states of functioning, if the conditions are suitable. Thus, even at the level of the 'deficiency needs', they would argue that the social worker is co-operating with an internally motivated process.

Practical objections

Let us now suppose that a group of social workers meet to discuss the relevance for their work and for their clients of the ideas set out so far. Some of them might show real interest and a wish to know more. Some would be sceptical, and others satirical and even scornful. These might say:

'There's not much wrong with most of my people that money wouldn't put right. How can I talk to a housewife about actualising herself when she's up to the ears in debt, there's no food in the house and the electricity's been cut off ...?'

'What about this unsupported mother? If she goes to bed with her man-friend she's actualising herself, isn't she? Tell that to the SBC when they cut off her benefit ...'

'My client was earning £45 per week as a steel erector until he had a fall. Now he's on sick pay, the car went first, the family's breaking up and he's going to lose his house. I can just hear what he'd say to you if you tell him to actualise himself out of that lot!'

These are very direct questions, and the answer is equally direct.

It is that the basis of life must be secured first, before it becomes possible to consider the quality of life, the reasons for living, or to have any choices at all.

It is a humiliating fact that our 'welfare state' in Britain does not provide welfare for all. Families that fall into great difficulties are astonished and bitter to discover how poor the service is, how little they can get from it. The basic problems of providing an adequate home, income, health service and education for all have not been solved. It is possible that the numbers of the deprived in Britain and America are increasing. The consequence is that social workers spend much of their time in basic welfare work, in coping with emergencies and in finding 'places' for clients—hospital beds, admission to a geriatric unit, and so on. Self-actualisation cannot develop on a basis of life-long enforced deprivation (—the chosen poverty of the priest or volunteer is a quite different matter). Maslow was always clear about this. He saw that the need for subsistence and security must be met before real relationships became possible and the self-development process was set in train.

'My clients are unemployed teenagers, many of them coloured. They come to me because of petty crimes, some of them violent.'

'I work with epileptics and discharged patients from a unit dealing with brain damage, often from car accidents. What these people cannot seem to find is stress-free work appropriate to their capacities.'

Work is the primary social means of self-expression in our society. It is the means whereby a man becomes accepted, and comes to accept himself. Work may be, and usually should be, transcended. A self-actualising man will feel himself to be more than a worker; but if he cannot get a job at all, he will feel less than a worker. Can a man without work actualise himself? Probably, but it is difficult. Sophisticated students sometimes decide to drop out and join the 'alternative society'. They experiment with communal living and casual earning for odd jobs, sometimes on partial self-employment. We need a new word for this—not unemployment, but non-employment, perhaps. We must hope that these young people will succeed in pioneering modes of existence in which relationship and self-acceptance are possible, so that our society is not simply structured into those whose lives are patterned by employment on the one hand, and those who are not wanted on the other.

'But my clients could never attain to such independence. Many of them are senile, or inadequate in some way, perhaps physically handicapped or mentally subnormal.'

It is among these that self-actualisation is most sharply observed. 'Institutionalisation', 'institutional neurosis'—such terms recognise the literally killing effects of placing people in settings where there is no space or function for the unique self. The other terms of our own day, 'therapeutic community', 'doing one's own thing', show an understanding of the need of apparently apathetic, anti-social, deteriorated people to become self-motivated again. A recent change in the living accommodation in an old people's home had this effect: before the change, nineteen of them were incontinent; after, only two. Yet such incontinence has been, and still is, often regarded as due to irreversible decline in the brain or nervous system.

'What then about clients who are really "psycho"? I have a boy who suffers from school phobia, he even faints when he gets near the classroom. Another client is wilfully cruel to his wife and child, and this seems clearly related to cruelty he experienced in his own childhood. Are not these problems better understood in Freudian terms?'

Freud gave us marvellously detailed studies of the complexity of factors and circumstances lying behind such problems. There is no need to discount any of his explanations, except that he phrased them in nineteenth-century mechanistic terms. He wrote as if a 'defence mechanism' were literally a mechanical system that some-how got going inside a person as a result of some trauma. His splendid observations have to be conserved and re-stated in terms of *personal* experience, and personal choice. If this is done, his writings become even more alive than they are as he presented them. A further depth of meaning is revealed when the clinical histories are seen in terms of a personal struggle for self-fulfilment; and when it is seen that self-fulfilment is the force that ultimately dissolves the neurosis. Freud knew this. His practice was better than his doctrine in this respect. He knew that psychoanalysis had nothing to say about mental health, and that this was a great deficiency. Self-actualisation supplies this missing dimension.

Self-love and self-actualisation

One of the basic problems in considering topics like the self, the self-concept, self-esteem and self-actualisation is the feeling that in so doing we are practising a form of narcissism or of selfishness. This feeling lies behind, I think, Frankl's criticisms of self-actualisation (see pp. 66-7 above). Classical psychoanalysis also in coupling its definition of the sexual perversion of narcissism with a secondary definition which includes any form of self-love has fostered the feeling that there is something wrong with self-love. The implication, however, behind the study of the self, in general, and in a concern with one's own self-development, in particular, is that there is nothing wrong with constructive self-concern.

Erich Fromm, always a constructive critic of psychoanalysis, has made a contribution to the debate. He says (1972, p. 47):

> The selfish person is interested only in himself, wants everything for himself, feels no pleasure in giving, but only in taking. The world outside is looked at only from the standpoint of what he can get out of it; he lacks interest in the needs of others, and respect for their dignity and integrity. He can see nothing but himself; he judges everyone and everything from its usefulness to him; he is basically unable to love.

If concern with one's self-development produced this sort of end-result, no case could be made out for it.

Fromm, in the passage quoted, is very concerned to make a basic distinction between selfishness and self-love. He asserts that *they are actually opposites*. The selfish person, in fact, does not love himself enough or care for himself enough. He is incapable of loving others but does not love himself either. His desire to obtain satisfactions for himself is, according to Fromm, an attempt to compensate for his failure to care for his real self. Tillich has suggested that the ambiguous term self-love be replaced by the phrase 'natural self-affirmation' in order to avoid confusion with what is, in fact, its opposite, i.e. selfishness. The psychoanalysts have taken to using the phrase 'healthy narcissism' to distinguish proper self-respect from 'over-valuation of the ego' (see Rycroft, 1968, p. 94).

Fromm, and others, therefore, are at pains to emphasise the

need for appropriate self-love. For example (Fromm, 1972, p. 48-9):

> If one has a chance to study the effect of a mother with genuine self-love, one can see that there is nothing more conducive to giving a child the experience of what love, joy and happiness are than being loved by a mother who loves herself.

This attitude to self-love is implicit, and sometimes explicit, in most of the thinkers referred to in this study of self-theory. Maslow's term is self-acceptance and he notes the absence of any sort of self-obsession. 'Our healthy individuals find it possible to accept themselves and their own nature without chagrin or complaint or, for that matter, even without thinking about the matter very much' (1954, p. 206).

It is necessary to underline this absence of self-obsession which Maslow has observed in his self-actualising subjects. It is clear from his report that the self-accepting person is not given to soul-searching in an anxious, worried way, but neither is he self-satisfied. He experiences, at times, guilt, shame, sadness, anxiety and defensiveness, but only about improveable shortcomings, remnants of prejudice and jealousy and old habits which are still strong; he accepts the realities of life, for example, his own needs, his own cultural background, and growing old.

Finally, the contrast we should make is not between self-love and the neurotic 'over-valuation of the ego', but between self-love and the widespread lack of self-concern by which individuals signify a lack of belief in their own potentiality and a tendency to regard themselves as a finished product. If a social worker does not see in himself a process of 'becoming' and development, then he is hardly likely to see his client creatively. Self-actualisation theory, therefore, is primarily a challenge to oneself.

Further reading

The two approaches to counselling which were selected for consideration in chapter 3 were those of Rogers and Frankl. The reader can study them further in the following texts:

FRANKL, V. E. (1969), *The Will to Meaning*, Souvenir Press.
ROGERS, C. R. (1965), *Client-Centred Therapy*, Houghton Mifflin.
ROGERS, C. R. (1967), *On Becoming a Person*, Constable.

There are many other distinctive approaches to counselling and the following titles are suggested as likely to be of value to the social work student.

BORDIN, E. S. (1968), *Psychological Counselling*, Appleton-Century-Crofts, 2nd edn.
> Written mainly for psychologists but useful for its emphasis on personality and role-choice.

GLASSER, W. (1965), *Reality Therapy*, Harper & Row.
> Written by a psychiatrist who has rejected Freudian 'reductionism' in favour of concentrating on the basic needs to love and be loved and to feel worthwhile to ourselves and others. Especially useful because it shows how therapeutic intentions can be combined with the disciplinary framework of an adolescent penal institution.

SCHOFIELD, W. (1964), *Psychotherapy: the purchase of friendship*, Prentice-Hall.
> Emphasises the importance of sympathy, listening ability and friendship *rather than* special techniques. The solution to today's needs is not to be found in 'professionalising' counselling but in the wider use of the counselling approach by people of all professions.

SHAW, JOHN (1973), *Basic Counselling*, Vernon Scott Associates.
> A step-by-step approach to the counselling interview. Emphasises counselling in organisational settings, but sufficiently basic to be of general usefulness.

WALLIS, J. H. (1973), *Personal Counselling: an introduction to relationship therapy*, Allen & Unwin.
> Emphasises the fact that beyond all the skills and knowledge one may possess, the quality of the relationship between the participants is the vital and healing element.

Bibliography

ALEN, ROBERT (1972), 'A personal relationship in intermediate treatment', *Social Service News*, vol. 2, no. 10, pp. 8-10.

ALLPORT, G. W. (1955), *Becoming: basic considerations for a psychology of personality*, Yale University Press.

ANDREWS, C. (1972), 'Intermediate treatment', *Social Service News*, vol. 2, no. 9, pp. 13-15.

ANGYAL, A. (1941), *Foundations for a Science of Personality*, Harvard University Press.

ARGYRIS, C. (1965), *Personality and Organisation*, Harper & Row.

ARGYRIS, C. (1969), *Interpersonal Competence and Organisational Effectiveness*, Irwin.

ARONSON, E. (1972), *The Social Animal*, W. H. Freeman.

ARTHUR, R. (1971), *An Introduction to Social Psychiatry*, Penguin.

ASCH, S. E. (1955), 'Opinions and social pressure', *Scientific American*, no. 193, pp. 31-5.

ASCH, S. E. (1956), 'Studies of independence and conformity', *Psychological Monographs*, no. 416.

BELBIN, R. M. (1969), *The Discovery Method*, OECD.

BERGER, P. and LUCKMANN, T. (1971), *The Social Construction of Reality*, Penguin.

BROMLEY, D. B. (1966), *The Psychology of Human Ageing*, Penguin.

BRUCH, H. (1948), 'Psychological aspects of obesity', *Bulletin of the New York Academy of Medicine*, vol. 24, pp. 73-86.

BÜHLER, C. (1933), *Der menschliche Lebenslauf als psychologisches Problem*, Leipzig.

CANNAN, C. (1972), 'Social workers; training and professionalism', in Pateman, T. (ed.), *Counter Course: a handbook for course criticism*, Penguin.

CATTELL, R. B. (1965), *The Scientific Analysis of Personality*, Penguin.

COAN, R. (1974), *The Optimal Personality*, Routledge & Kegan Paul.

COFER, C. N. and APPLEY, M. H. (1964), *Motivation: theory and research*, Wiley.

COOLEY, C. H. (1902), *Human Nature and the Social Order*, Scribner.
DUNNETTE, M. and CAMPBELL, J. (1968), 'Effectiveness of T-Group experiences in managerial training and development', *Psychological Bulletin*, vol. 70, pp. 73-104.
ERIKSON, E. (1963), *Childhood and Society*, Norton, 2nd edn.
FRANKL, V. E. (1969a), *The Doctor and the Soul*, Souvenir Press.
FRANKL, V. E. (1969b), *The Will to Meaning*, Souvenir Press.
FRICK, W. B. (1971), *Humanistic Psychology; interviews with Maslow, Murphy, and Rogers*, Merrill.
FROMM, E. (1972), *The Art of Loving*, Allen & Unwin.
GOFFMAN, E. (1968), *Stigma*, Penguin.
GOLDSTEIN, K. (1939), *The Organism*, American Book Co.
HOLMBERG, A. R. (1950), *Nomads of the Long Bow: the Siriono of Eastern Bolivia*, Smithsonian Institute.
JACOBI, J. (1967), *The Way of Individuation*, Hodder & Stoughton.
JAFFÉ, A. (ed.) (1963), *C. G. Jung: memories, dreams and reflections*, Collins and Routledge & Kegan Paul.
JAHODA, M. (1958), *Current Concepts of Positive Mental Health*, Basic Books.
JOURARD, S. (1964), *The Transparent Self*, Van Nostrand.
JUNG, C. G. (1958a), *The Undiscovered Self*, Routledge & Kegan Paul.
JUNG, C. G. (1958b), *Psychology and Religion, Collected Works*, vol. II, Routledge & Kegan Paul.
JUNG, C. G. (1968), *Analytical Psychology*, Routledge & Kegan Paul.
KELLEY, C. R. (1971), 'Education in feeling and purpose', *Energy and Character*, vol. 2, no. 1, pp. 52-69.
KEYS, A. *et al.* (1950), *The Biology of Human Starvation*, University of Minnesota Press.
LEONARD, P. (1966), *Sociology in Social Work*, Routledge & Kegan Paul.
LEWIN, K. (1952), 'Group decision and social change' in Swanson, G. E., Newcomb, T. H. and Hartley, E. L. (eds) (1952), *Readings in Social Psychology*, Holt, Rinehart & Winston.
LOMAS, P. (1965), 'Family interaction and the sick role' in Wisdom, J. O. and Wolff, H. H. (eds.), *The Role of the Psychosomatic Disorder in Adult Life*, Pergamon.
MASLOW, A. H. (1954), *Motivation and Personality*, Harper & Row.
MASLOW, A. H. (1968), *Towards a Psychology of Being*, Van Nostrand.
MASLOW, A. H. (1973), *The Farther Reaches of Human Nature*, Penguin: includes 'The fusion of facts and values' (1963), 'Theory Z' (1969), and 'A theory of meta-motivation: The biological rooting of the value life' (1967).
MAY, ROLLO (1967), *Man's Search for Himself*, New American Library.
RASKIN, N. J. (1952), 'An objective study of the locus of evaluation factor in psychotherapy' in Wolff, W. and Precker, J. A. (eds), *Success in Psychotherapy*, Grune & Stratton.
REICH, W. (1969), *Character Analysis*, Vision Press.
REICHARD, S. *et al.* (1962), *Ageing and Personality: a study of eighty-seven older men*, Wiley.
ROGERS, C. R. (1946), 'Significant aspects of client-centred therapy',

American Psychologist, vol. 1, pp. 415-22.

ROGERS, C. R. (1965), *Client-Centred Therapy*, Houghton Mifflin.

ROGERS, C. R. (1967), *On Becoming a Person*, Constable.

ROGERS, C. R. (1969), 'The group comes of age', *Psychology Today*, December.

ROGERS, C. R. (1971), *Encounter Groups*, Allen Lane, Penguin.

ROGERS, C. R. and DYMOND, R. F. (eds) (1954), *Psychotherapy and Personality Change*, University of Chicago Press.

RUBIN, I. (1967), 'The reduction of prejudice through laboratory training', *Journal of Applied Behavioural Science*, vol. 3, pp. 29-50.

RUDDOCK, R. (1969), *Roles and Relationships*, Routledge & Kegan Paul.

RUDDOCK, R. (1972), 'Conditions of personal identity', in Ruddock (ed.), *Six Approaches to the Person*, Routledge & Kegan Paul.

RYCROFT, C. (1968), *A Critical Dictionary of Psychoanalysis*, Nelson.

SCHACHTEL, E. G. (1959), *Metamorphosis*, Basic Books.

SCHUTZ, W. (1973), *Joy: expanding human awareness*, Penguin.

SHAW, JOHN (1972), 'The personal imperative: a study of the evidence for self-actualisation', in Ruddock (ed.), *Six Approaches to the Person*.

SZASZ, T. (1961), *The Myth of Mental Illness*, Routledge & Kegan Paul.

TEN HAVE, T. T. (1973), 'Andragogy in later life', paper presented to the SCUTREA conference.

WALLIS, J. H. (1973), *Personal Counselling: an introduction to relationship therapy*, Allen & Unwin.

WHYTE, W. H. (1956), *The Organisation Man*, Simon & Schuster.

WOLFF, H. H. (1965), 'Why do emotional conflicts express themselves in physical symptoms?', in Wisdom, J. O. and Wolff, H. H. (eds), *The Role of Psychosomatic Disorder in Adult Life*, Pergamon.